'D' is for DONKEY

Dr Svendsen on the last day of Donkey Week 9th May 2011.

DR ELISABETH SVENDSEN MBE

23RD JANUARY 1930 – 11TH MAY 2011

On 11th May my dear mother passed away suddenly. Right up to her last moments she was doing what she loved – caring for animals and writing about how important they were in her life. I am so pleased that she finished writing this book in the last few weeks, although sorry that she will not see it in print. It is, however, a wonderful reminder of her caring nature and her love of donkeys and all animals. We, her family, friends, staff and donkeys will miss her terribly, but she will live on in our hearts and through her books forever.

PAUL SVENDSEN

'D' is for DONKEY

An A to Z of Donkey Facts and Stories

DR ELISABETH D SVENDSEN MBE

Kenilworth Press

First published in the UK in 2011
by Kenilworth Press, an imprint of Quiller Publishing Ltd

British Library Cataloguing-in-Publication Data
A catalogue record for this book
is available from the British Library

ISBN 978 1 905693 39 9

Designed and typeset by Paul Saunders

Printed in China

Kenilworth Press
An imprint of Quiller Publishing Ltd
Wykey House, Wykey, Shrewsbury, SY4 1JA
Tel: 01939 261616 Fax: 01939 261606
E-mail: info@quillerbooks.com
Website: www.kenilworthpress.co.uk

Dedication

This book is dedicated to Sue Harland, who has worked with me
for many years and without whose excellent help many of my numerous
books would never have been written. Thank you, Sue, and have a
long and happy retirement!

INTRODUCTION

Wandering in my mind through the alphabet for this book has led me to thinking back over the years and realising how acquiring two little donkeys became the start of a whole new way of life for me. Little did I know then that my future would revolve almost entirely around the care and welfare of donkeys in need. Having started my own small family of donkeys in 1969, I established The Donkey Sanctuary in 1973, and this has been of enormous benefit to millions of donkeys both in the UK and throughout the world. The Sanctuary's work for donkeys overseas is, in turn, helping their impoverished owners, who rely on their animals for their everyday livelihood. As well as this charity I founded The Elisabeth Svendsen Trust for Children and Donkeys, which gives children with special educational needs and disabilities the opportunity to ride and have close contact with donkeys in six custom-built Centres throughout the UK. The two donkeys who started it all were Angelina and Naughty Face!

The story really started when I was five years old. Every third weekend my parents, with my sister Pat and me, travelled from our home in Elland, Yorkshire, to St Annes-on-Sea in Lancashire to visit my grandparents. The journey in my father's little Hillman (JX 1930 was the registration number) was never a comfortable one, particularly as in 1935 many of Yorkshire's roads were cobbled! There was, however, a reason I looked forward to the journey. If I begged and pleaded hard enough my father would agree to make a five mile detour through Hebden Bridge. There, in a field, were two donkeys! As soon as the car stopped, I would rush out and run up to the fence at the top of a bank. I would shout 'Donkeys!' and, without fail, they would trot over to me for a cuddle! I think my love of these delightful animals began then.

I was so lucky to have a loving family, who nursed me through some unfortunate illnesses, which ultimately resulted in my contracting osteomyelitis. This nearly cost me my right arm and resulted in permanent damage to my hand, which to this day causes me difficulties at times. However, I was able to attend Teacher Training College and obtained a 1st Class Froebel degree. I found that my primary interest was in children with special needs and I spent some time while at college at the Fountain Hospital for mentally ill children in the Deptford area of London.

My teaching career ceased when my father's secretary died. She had been running the office in his sanitary pipe works for many years, and I was persuaded to take her place. My father explained, 'Ee lass, Fanny Sutcliffe has worked for me for forty-five years and we don't want any strangers knowing our business!'

I needed to take a crash course in typing and accountancy and was soon tackling wages for sixty miners on different rates of pay, and fettlers on piece work! I often wandered down the yards where the kilns were belching out flames and, when asking my father 'why is there a large water butt by each kiln?' he shocked me by explaining that they were for the men to douse the flames should their clothes catch fire – which they often did!

Sometimes I had to drive one of the six-ton lorries for emergency deliveries. In the days of double de-clutching this was quite a feat and, if I had to brake suddenly, it was alarming to hear the pipes thumping against the back of the cab window. Many of the deliveries were to building sites and I caused quite a stir on arrival, as they didn't expect a woman driver!

I met Niels Svendsen and we married in 1954. At that time Niels was working with his brother building up their company, 'Metalife'. I was able to help out in my spare time – you can't imagine how many chimneys we painted with anti-corrosive paint in the West Riding of Yorkshire! A disagreement with his brother led to Niels taking a job with British Cellophane at Bridgwater in Somerset, which meant moving house. I found this rather difficult, as I had to leave my job and by then had my first baby, Lise.

At first, and with another baby on the way, we rented a flat near Bridgwater, and it was here that we encountered a big problem – we were not allowed to hang washing outside! I got quite desperate after Paul joined Lise; I had two children under fifteen months old with the resultant laundry problems. Together Niels and I came up with the idea of an electrically powered nappy drier! Niels built them in a rented shed and I went out selling them with my two babies in the back of the car! It was hard work, but successful. One day in 1958 we saw an article in the *News Chronicle* advertising a 'Get Ahead' competition. There was nothing to lose and so we entered our nappy drier. The finals were televised and to our great delight, we won! We were awarded the (then) magnificent sum of £5,000 and gained enormous publicity! Within three days the demand was so great for our driers that Niels resigned from his job and we set up a factory and employed nationwide salesmen. While exhibiting at the Ideal Homes Exhibition in 1961 we were approached by one of the Directors of Thorn Electrical Industries, who made us such a tempting offer we decided to sell our business to the company while still remaining as directors of one of its branches. However, after being his own boss, Niels wasn't enjoying being employed and so after two years of good salaries and a Bentley as a company car we gave it all up to become business consultants!

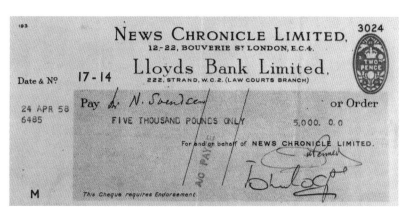

Invitation to the final of the 'Get Ahead' competition

The winning cheque!

Our first job was in Cornwall, putting a shipyard back on its feet, but after a few years Niels' recurring back problems forced us to think again and, with three young children to consider (Clive was born in May 1961), we decided we would buy and run a hotel, so there would always be plenty of help if Niels' bad back meant he couldn't work. I went to look at the Salston Hotel in Ottery St Mary, which was for sale with four acres of land.

As I gazed at the lovely field in front of the hotel I remembered the donkeys I'd loved during my childhood and I could imagine donkeys happily grazing there. So, we bought the Salston Hotel and in 1969 Naughty Face arrived!

I loved Naughty Face, but after a while she showed obvious signs of being very lonely – the hotel residents didn't seem to appreciate her mournful brays day and night! A companion was needed urgently and the problem was solved when Angelina joined us.

This book tells the stories of many of the donkeys that The Donkey Sanctuary has cared for, either by taking them into its care or through the work which is being carried out for hundreds of thousands of donkeys both in the UK and abroad. They are in alphabetical, not date, order – hence the title of the book.

Although not strictly in order I feel that Angelina must come first in section A of this book, as she and Naughty Face were where it all began…

A is for Apple

A is for apple that donkeys adore
B is for breakfast – they always want more
C is for cold, when abandoned and lost
D is for Donkey Sanctuary – we don't count the cost.

This book is for you, to read and enjoy
To realise a donkey is not just a toy
But alive, giving help to all that they meet
From poorest peasant, to man in the street.

We've tried to connect them from A through to Z
It's the sort of book you can take to your bed;
It covers the world and what donkeys can do
And brings tears, and joy, from me to you!

Dr Elisabeth D Svendsen 2010

DONKEYS

Angelina

I think one of the first lessons I learned about donkeys is that they don't like living alone. Naughty Face, my first donkey, had been so lonely living on her own and her braying had regularly woken our hotel guests, so I decided to buy another donkey to keep her company. Angelina was a beautiful chocolate brown donkey with a lovely nature to match and, like Naughty Face, she was in foal. They got on together splendidly.

Unfortunately, despite my best efforts and those of the vet, Angelina's foal was born dead, which was heartbreaking for us all. However, she quickly recovered and helped look after Naughty Face's little foal, Superdocious. From then on Angelina was in charge!

In 1970 we had been fortunate enough to be able to buy a house with four bedrooms at the bottom of a lane close to the hotel, which proved ideal for my family as well as the donkeys, as there were stables and, like the hotel, it had four acres of land. My idea of starting a stud farm was taking shape.

I bought a beautiful stallion, St Paddy of Kennetbury, and Angelina was definitely number one wife! It was she who calmed St Paddy down when he had a bad experience with a television crew from the local BBC news programme, 'Spotlight'. The presenter, Bob Forbes, set the scene for a feature on the 'Donkey Lady' and despite my protests, he insisted on filming in St Paddy's paddock. Angelina was with St Paddy to keep him in order!

Unfortunately for the cameraman he was wearing a full length brown, hairy Afghan coat – I say unfortunately because St Paddy, who was watching the proceedings with great interest, was at the edge of the paddock directly behind him. Bob started asking me questions. I was gently scratching Angelina's ears and trying to answer the questions calmly but, out of the corner of my eye I could see St Paddy, whose ears were flat against his head and he was pawing at the ground with his hoof. He'd obviously decided that the cameraman, as he crouched over the camera, was a visiting mare! All of a sudden St Paddy moved like lightning and suddenly there was utter chaos! Poor St Paddy received a great shock, as his 'mare' collapsed under him and Angelina sprang forward to see what all the fuss was about. Angelina nudged and pushed at St Paddy and, between us, we were able to quieten him down. They were both returned to their stable and that was the end of filming for the day. I met the cameraman again several months later. He told me he would never wear the coat again – I wasn't surprised!

Angelina was in foal to St Paddy when I stopped breeding donkeys, having become deeply concerned over the fate of many donkeys in the UK. She safely produced a darling little colt, who I named Russell (of whom more later in the book).

After many happy years at the Sanctuary Angelina died in 1997. Of course, I always feel sad to lose any of our donkeys, but Angelina was so very special to me and I missed her enormously. Unfortunately I no longer have a photograph of her.

Alfred

One of the donkeys collected from Miss Philpin's (see her story under 'P') sanctuary after her death was one I named 'Alfred' after Alfred the Great. At that time he was the biggest donkey we had taken into care and, apart from his hooves, which were badly in need of a trim, he was in fairly good condition Although large, he could be described as almost elegant! He had excellent manners, always carried himself well and was a perfect gentleman with the farrier!

Shortly after his arrival my ideas for putting children with special needs and donkeys together for their mutual benefit got under way and Alfred, partly because of his size and partly because of his good manners, was chosen for the trial. He proved absolutely wonderful. The children loved him and he adored the children!

In those days, before we built The Slade Centre, we would take the donkeys out to the children at their schools. The children shrieked with joy when they saw the donkeys coming down the ramp at the back of the lorry – to many of them it was the highlight of their week. The children's joy turned to sadness in the winter when the rides had to stop but, in December 1978 The Slade Centre opened, with its super play area and riding arena designed for the comfort of donkeys and children alike. Now the rides take place all year round.

Alfred was always a great favourite with everyone and his compassion and understanding knew no bounds. One day, Alfred was the second in line of five donkeys giving rides to a group of severely disabled children. One of the many games we use had been set up, and propped against the rail on the left hand side of the arena were a number of envelopes, with a letterbox on the opposite side. The children, on donkey back, had to stop the donkey, pick up the letter, ride around the arena and post it in the letterbox. Alfred's rider was severely handicapped and, despite very real attempts the child could not pick up the envelope. After he had failed at the third attempt, Alfred turned his head round and grasped the envelope firmly in his teeth. Then to everyone's amazement,

Alfred and me!

he carried his rider to the letterbox and stopped with the envelope only inches from the hole! Who says donkeys aren't intelligent?

Alicia

Alicia's mother, Nana, was in foal and had a severe hoof problem when she was taken into care at El Refugio del Burrito in Spain. Although she continues to be monitored, the degeneration of her pedal bones in her feet still causes her a great deal of pain. Painkillers and anti-inflammatory drugs are helping but her prognosis is not good. Despite her problems, on Mother's Day in 2009 she gave birth to a beautiful foal, who we called Alicia.

Alicia's first birthday was celebrated in May 2010 at her home at Fuente de Piedra, the main farm of El Refugio del Burrito in Spain. The staff made a lot of fuss of her, and gave her a little treat – a luscious carrot cake! Hopefully this will be the first birthday of many more in a safe, loving environment; she is a lucky donkey to have known only love and care from day one. She is a happy little donkey and is now living with other female donkeys. Her new friends are Celia, Pepa, Canela, Romera and Romina.

Alicia at her birthday party

Ashley

In June 2009 we received an urgent request to take into our care eight donkeys from the north-west of Scotland. The donkeys were in need of a new home due to a change in the owner's circumstances. The donkeys arrived safely and, after they'd had a good night's rest our vets carried out the usual routine medical checks. They found that four of the mares were in foal! One of them, Maible, gave birth within two weeks of her arrival, producing a delightful colt foal who we named Brian, in memory of a former member of staff who had died a few weeks previously. A second mare, Flora, gave birth to her foal, Zena (see her story under 'Z'), a few weeks later.

Sadly things did not go well for another of the new arrivals, Aisling. She suffered a fatal complication during the birth and, despite desperate efforts by our staff, we lost her. The little colt foal was weak and we knew it was quite possible we could lose him as well. It really was a desperate situation; Ashley needed feeding every two hours day and night, which was exhausting for the members of staff from various departments who volunteered to help. Elena, one of our vets, was in charge of looking after him. After a few days she said, 'Ashley is a delightful little character and every day goes from strength to strength He is responding better than I had expected, so I'm really pleased.' After two weeks other members of staff, including office members, volunteered to help the veterinary team and they found their days and nights changed beyond recognition! Thankfully, with skilful care Ashley hung on and, after a month, we knew he had turned the corner. It was relief all round!

Ashley, orphaned at birth

Hand-reared foals can, however, develop poor behavioural characteristics; the staff had to be careful to minimise cuddles because he could otherwise grow to prefer humans to donkeys – it was so hard to resist the temptation, though! So during the day Ashley was put into a paddock with Flora and Zena. Flora looked after him well and taught him how good donkeys should behave!

DONKEY FACTS, PEOPLE AND PLACES

Abbie

Abbie has been attending EST Manchester from the time she began to sit unaided at around two years old. She has gained both in self-confidence and riding skills. When she first came she was just able to sit and her feet didn't even reach the stirrups, but she has progressed through our achievement levels in all aspects of therapy, including her language development. One of the Centre's riding instructors, Robina, says, 'Abbie has really come out of herself! She used to be so shy in any communication, but now she always comes in with a big smile on her face, tells me about her day at school and makes sure she has her drink and flapjack.'

One of the real bonuses in learning to ride our donkeys has been the improvement in Abbie's self-esteem. Robina goes onto say, 'Abbie is now learning all the "real skills" of riding, using her reins and "steering". It is so rewarding to see that as she has matured she has also begun to learn how to take care of our donkeys.'

Abbie likes helping wherever she can!

Abbie's mother, Julie, can't stress too greatly how much the donkeys are a part of her life. Abbie recently attended a speech and language course with horse riding and was able to ride with confidence and transfer the skills she has acquired from donkey riding. Julie says she can't praise the staff at EST Manchester enough for the support, interest and pleasure they have given her.

Abigail

Donkey riding therapy has been instrumental in helping Abigail to learn to walk and find a new sense of self-confidence. At the age of two she was not yet able to crawl and struggled with a range of developmental delays that prevented her from interacting with children and adults outside of her family. She had low muscle tone and learning difficulties which caused problems with her balance and her ability to walk.

Abigail has now been attending the EST Leeds Centre for three years and has amazed her family with the improvements that the riding sessions have made. Her mother, Carol, recalls:

'Abigail was very withdrawn and wouldn't interact with other children or join in with their activities or games, but since we began coming to EST I have seen enormous changes in what she is able to achieve. The riding sessions are tailored to include activities that focus on developing Abigail's core strength and flexibility. Her physiotherapist is delighted with the improvements in her muscle tone, mobility and posture – she is now able to run around like every other child, which is wonderful to see.'

Abigail can now use the stirrups to climb onto the donkey, hold the reins during riding, and she engages with the educational elements of each session, such as naming colours and matching pictures together. She now interacts with the other children and has managed to form strong friendships.

Abigail often rides with her sister, Isabelle, at the Saturday Clubs and in the school holidays. Carol says: 'It's brilliant that the girls can do an activity together that they both enjoy. Abigail is always excited about visiting the Centre and asks if it's "donkeys today" on most days!'

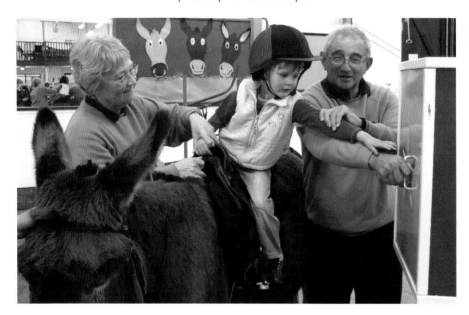

Abigail enjoying her donkey riding games

Adoption Scheme

The Elisabeth Svendsen Trust for Children and Donkeys (EST) offers supporters the opportunity to choose a donkey from one of its Centres that can be classed as their 'special' donkey. The main aspects of the Adoption Scheme are:

- A choice of twenty-four donkeys, four of each at Belfast, Birmingham, Ivybridge, Leeds, Manchester and Sidmouth.
- Those who adopt will receive a folder, certificate, details of the adopted donkey, a colour picture and a beautiful A4 pencil drawing. An update on the chosen donkey is sent every six months.
- A donkey can be adopted on behalf of any person as a gift. A personal message can be included.
- More details can be obtained by email: www.elisabethsvendsentrust.org.uk/adoptions, or by telephone: 01395 573034.

DONKEYS

Barney

Barney was a contender for the title of 'the naughtiest donkey at the Sanctuary'. In fact he was one of the reasons we had to buy a new donkey lorry! He was bought in a market in Wales by a concerned donkey lover, who saw that he was in a terrible state, having lice and poor feet, as well as a large cancerous growth (known as a sarcoid) on his inside hind leg. Once satisfied that he had recovered sufficiently to travel, Barney was signed over to us and he was collected in our lorry. What a journey! Despite desperate efforts by the driver, Barney proceeded methodically to rip all the protective panels from the sides of the lorry. By the time he arrived at the Sanctuary the driver was nearing a nervous breakdown, but Barney had experienced the time of his life! As he was a stallion he was castrated and put in the stallion yard for his six week isolation period. Nothing was safe – wheelbarrows were tipped over, staff were playfully pushed around, brooms were picked up and swung around – there was no end to his tricks. He was, however, really popular with all the staff. When his isolation period was over we had to put Barney with the Poitou donkeys (where he remains to this day), who are large enough to stand up for themselves and, with a big blue football they keep themselves amused for hours on end.

Barney (reproduced with the kind permission of Jim Wileman)

Beau

Beau arrived at the Donkey Sanctuary (Cyprus) in 2005 aged eight years. He had been abandoned in a village near Limassol and was found eating beans belonging to a rather irate farmer! He had two nasty large wounds on his face which were treated by the vet. Beau is an unusual colour for a donkey in Cyprus – more of a typical Eastern European donkey – grey, with a well-defined cross on his back. He is a cheeky, strong chap who enjoys chewing the grooms' shirts while they are cleaning his paddock. The only thing he isn't too keen on is having his back hooves trimmed, but as he is so handsome we can forgive him for that!

He continues to be as mischievous as ever, but was a paragon of virtue when he had his teeth checked and rasped recently, and his behaviour is slowly improving with the farrier. He is available for adoption under the Donkey Sanctuary (Cyprus) Adoption Scheme.

Beau

Ben

Ben belonged to an English owner who unfortunately was too busy to look after him. He was eight years old when he came into the Donkey Sanctuary (Cyprus) in 2003 and a very handsome and strong donkey he is! He likes being around people and we are sure he knows how good looking he is, as he seems to like to pose for photographs.

Ben is a very happy little chap who appreciates lots of fuss and cuddles, and he enjoys being a member of the Donkey Sanctuary (Cyprus) Adoption Scheme.

Ben

Bill and Ben (1)

It is very rare for a donkey to have twins – in fact I've only heard of about six sets in the last thirty years, one of which was exceptionally rare – twins born to a Poitou donkey in Germany. However, in 2003 we welcomed Bill and Ben (formerly known as Ronnie and Reggie) from Wales. Sadly their owner's health and personal problems made it necessary for them to be relinquished into our care.

The twins are a perfectly matched pair and, as they have never been apart, they are closely bonded with each other. It was particularly touching to see the twins had brought with them their own 'feed bowl' which they had shared all their lives and which their owner felt would serve as a 'comforter'! They stand at eleven hands high, which is quite large and according to their owner they are 'desperate to be busy'.

It was soon obvious that they both loved interacting with people, especially children, so we decided they should join our Education and Activities Department (E & A). These donkeys are taken to visit schools, as well as taking part in the educational projects we arrange for children visiting the Sanctuary.

Bill and Ben are delightful donkeys, constantly keeping the staff on their toes! They always have to be involved in everything that is going on, and will tug at the grooms' clothes if they think they're being ignored. They love helping the grooms as they clean their shelter and yard, and have been known to grab the brush and the large 'scooper' pan (one each!) and clatter around the yard, quite determined to dodge their carers, Jan and Sue! They also love playing football and undoing coat zips – particularly if they can smell polo mints!

One evening, on my daily walk, I was very concerned to find Bill on the wrong side of the fence. This meant he couldn't get back to his warm stable for the night. I had no head collar with me and, as I rushed back to the main buildings I realised most of the staff would have left, as it was getting late. There were three voluntary workers in the EST Centre, who kindly offered to help but, as they didn't know Bill, I decided to see if there was anyone else around who could go with them. I was delighted when I found Maggie in the Visitors'

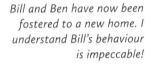

Bill and Ben have now been fostered to a new home. I understand Bill's behaviour is impeccable!

Centre! Maggie knew all the donkeys at Slade House Farm, and I was pleased to accept her offer to go with the volunteers, particularly as she was familiar with the electric fence and would be able to turn it off. They set off without me, as the shelter was a fair distance away and it was now pitch dark. I was pleased to learn the next day that they had succeeded in their task.

The story doesn't end there, however. A couple of days later Maggie went out with a few ginger nuts in her hand to give the other donkeys a treat before taking them out for a visit to a school. Once again, Bill was on the wrong side of the fence. When he saw the biscuits in Maggie's hand, to her amazement he took a short run and jumped cleanly over the fence with no trouble. The fence was nearly three feet high – none of us had realised that donkeys were able to jump that high voluntarily – and the lure of the biscuits was just too much temptation! I kept thinking of my desperate rush a few days earlier to ensure we could help Bill round the fence so that he could get into his warm stable for the night, but I now realised that he must have jumped over in the first place. The grass was obviously greener on that side!

Bill and Ben (2)

In 2010 another pair of twins came into the Sanctuary – coincidentally with the same names. They had been owned by the Cotswold Rare Breed Farm Park and were purchased by a lady from Tiverton, who kept them for nine years. Unfortunately she lost her grazing land, so she relinquished the donkeys to us.

Bill and Ben are very closely bonded – so much so that they become very agitated even if only separated by a gate.

Bill and Ben enjoying life at East Axnoller Farm

Bill, Ben and Boots

Bill, Ben and Boots arrived at the Sanctuary in 1973 and were the first donkeys to be rehabilitated to a 'foster home'. An elderly lady contacted us to say that she and her two sisters were willing to offer a good home to three donkeys. My sister, Pat, arranged to visit the three ladies and was most impressed by the enormous house standing in beautiful grounds with fenced paddocks, walled gardens and a large stable block complete with groom and stable boy, although there had been no horses there for about fifteen years!

In August Bill, Ben and Boots were taken to their new home, where they were greeted with all the love and attention they could wish for. I telephoned a few days later to find that everything was going well; each sister had her own favourite and the donkeys were as good as gold. I continued to phone on regular occasions over the next few months and there were no problems.

I was, therefore, very surprised to receive a telephone call that November. 'Mrs Svendsen, I'm sorry, but you must take Bill and Ben back. They've become such naughty boys. Boots can stay, as he's so good, but we just cannot cope with the other two!' 'I'm so sorry,' I said. 'Whatever are they up to?' 'Well,' said the lady,' they have become so disobedient. Boots goes straight up the stairs when we tell him but, no matter how we push and pull, Bill and Ben refuse to go up. You know we are elderly ladies, Mrs Svendsen, and we can't do such heavy work.' 'Did you say up the stairs?' I asked. 'Of course … you don't think we can lie upstairs in our warm beds at night and leave those three in the stables, do you? It gets cold, you know – they use the guest bedroom.'

So Bill and Ben came back to us, followed one month later by Boots, who ceased to be angelic when his friends departed!

Blackie Star and Lola

Blackie was probably the Sanctuary's most famous donkey! In 1986 we heard of an annual fiesta which took place on Shrove Tuesday in Villanueva de la Vera, a town in the Extremadura region of Spain. Each year a procession takes place which includes a donkey being ridden by a man who is far too heavy and is usually drunk. A thick rope with knots tied in it is put around the donkey's neck and the poor animal is dragged along by men holding onto the knots, urged on by hundreds of over-excited onlookers. Reports were that the donkey used that year had fallen and been crushed to death by the crowd.

Vicki Moore, an animal rights campaigner (who died in 2000 after battling for several years to recover from injuries sustained during one of her protests) offered to attend the 1987 fiesta if the Sanctuary would pay her expenses. The press had been notified and Vicki was accompanied by reporters from several newspapers, including the *Sun* and the *Star*. Vicki confirmed that the treatment of the donkey was appalling; he fell several times, only to be dragged back to its feet again; he was punched and kicked and terrified by the shouts of the crowd and the sounds of guns being fired into the air. Although the donkey, who the locals called Blackie, survived, he was in great distress after the event. It was arranged that the *Star* would buy him, provided we could bring him back to the Sanctuary and that he would bear the newspaper's name.

It proved to be difficult rescuing Blackie, but John Fowler (the Sanctuary's vet at the time) and I, accompanied by two reporters from the *Star*, set off four weeks after the event with a small Sanctuary lorry. The villagers had hidden him, but one animal lover took pity on us and we were guided to his hiding place. We carefully loaded him onto the lorry and travelled to the ferry port at Santander. We had to put the lorry on the car deck, but the captain kindly allowed us to enter at regular intervals to feed, water and comfort him.

When we arrived at Plymouth we managed to get him to the Sanctuary before the two reporters released the news. Blackie arrived in the UK amid huge media interest and we received literally thousands of visitors, who came to see the famous donkey from Spain. He was settled into what we call the 'Salston Box' with its own little paddock, accompanied by a new donkey companion, Lola, who had arrived from Wales at the same time. Blackie and Lola thoroughly enjoyed all the attention they received, although Blackie was rather reticent – possibly because of his ordeal, or probably because he didn't understand English!

A team from the Sanctuary has attended the fiesta every year since then to see what help can be given to the poor donkey used. Accompanied by a vet I visited on the first three occasions to witness how much suffering the donkey

A Christmas photo of the three of us!

endured. It was very frightening for us and the donkey, as 12-bore shotguns were being fired at random all the time. We have tried many things over the years to stop this dreadful practice, including presenting a petition with over 25,000 signatures to the Spanish Ambassador in London, offering a life-sized model donkey to the town as a replacement for a real donkey and many attempts to persuade the Spanish authorities to legislate against the use of live animals in fiestas. Despite all our political and practical efforts, however, it still continues to this day.

Blackie spent seven happy years at The Donkey Sanctuary before, probably as a result of the abuse he had suffered in his early years, he died in May 1993. Having spent an hour with Blackie after he died (our normal practice in the event of the death of a donkey companion), Lola was able to accept the fact that he was gone and, after being moved to New Barn in the main yard she soon found a new companion – a twenty-six year old skewbald donkey named Mumphrey!

Boomer

Boomer's owner had suffered a car accident and could no longer care for him, so he was taken into our care. As he is such a gentle, friendly donkey it was decided that he should be trained to work with children with special needs and dis-

advantages who attend our EST Centres. He was chosen as one of the team of donkeys that moved to the Ivybridge Centre in March 2007.

Bob Venn, Principal of the Centre says: 'Boomer has been a very busy donkey since he's been with us. From the moment he arrived, he played an important role in the opening of Christmas grottos in a superstore in Plymouth, joining a procession bringing Father Christmas and his helpers into the grotto in a carriage. He also had a lot of media interest when his duties took on a distinctive 'military' feel. Each year in the Royal Citadel on Plymouth Hoe, where 29 Commando Royal Artillery is based, a concert is held called 'The Music of the Night'. The concert features the massed bands of Her Majesty's Royal Marines and hundreds of singers, dancers and actors. It runs for six nights, and is watched by over three thousand people each night. In 2007 one of the sets featured Joseph and his Amazing Technicolour Dreamcoat. EST Ivybridge was asked to provide a donkey, and Boomer appeared on all six nights. He was a true star – he thoroughly enjoyed all of the fuss and attention made of him and was completely unconcerned by all the noise – in particular the loud fireworks! He got a huge cheer each night, which he seemed to appreciate!

Boomer

Unfortunately Boomer developed a knee joint problem which resulted in him requiring arthroscopic examination and treatment of the joint. He was referred to Western Counties Equine Clinic for a specialist procedure. After surgery Boomer was discharged to recuperate at The Donkey Sanctuary hospital, where he needed a prolonged stay to be given intensive medication, as well as physiotherapy. Happily he made a good recovery and was able to return to EST Ivybridge. What a welcome he received from his donkey friends!

Buffalo

Buffalo must have been one of the biggest donkeys around – and he certainly must have had the biggest ears! Thousands of years ago, when donkeys and horses lived wild in Africa and Asia, the stronger horses tended to push the donkeys off the richer pastures, so the donkeys took to the hills and mountains where, although the grazing was much poorer, they could at least graze peacefully. This made communication difficult and it appears to be the reason for the donkey's penetrating voice to call with and large ears to hear with. If this is so, then Buffalo could go up the highest mountain and still hear his friends!

Buffalo, one of my all-time favourites!

He came to us in September 1977 and was the 457th entry. He arrived with three friends, Blupy, Bonanza and Bobby; all had been working on Blackpool beach for (excuse the expression) donkeys' years and were now in their thirties. Their owner decided they deserved a happy retirement. When the lorry doors opened I couldn't believe the size of Buffalo. His feet were over twice the size of the average donkey's and, as my eyes went upwards, there was the most enormous shaggy body, crowned with a superb head and the most enormous ears!

Every new arrival at the Sanctuary is given a name and number and, at the time of Buffalo's arrival, we were buying made up 'cow collars'. 'Goodness!' I muttered as I tried in vain to get the collar around his huge neck. 'He really is the size of a buffalo.' Actually he did us a great favour, as we rang the manufacturers of the collars and we were able to buy the collar material in rolls, which was much cheaper and could be made up to fit the necessary neck size.

Buffalo was such a softy – it's almost impossible to describe him. When he was being groomed and you bent down to brush his legs he slowly began to lean on you, with a beatific expression on his face! Only the strongest could take his weight and I certainly don't qualify for that, usually collapsing in an undignified heap to be nudged up by Buffalo with an enquiring expression on his face.

The first time our farrier saw him he put down his file and slowly walked about him with a delighted grin on his face. 'Now that's what I call a donkey,' he said. 'Not half so far to bend down as usual, but is he good?' He soon found out. Buffalo enjoyed his pedicure thoroughly and stood patiently, even lifting his enormous feet towards the farrier as he bent to his task.

Buffalo's only problem seemed to be the enormous size of his ears. When he got tired the muscle needed to hold them up seemed to sag and, slowly, like great handlebars, first one ear collapsed, then the other, until finally they drooped at right angles to his head! His size, though, gave him an advantage; in the stable he could happily stand in the second row behind one of the smaller donkeys in his group, and was able to casually lean over and help himself over the top of the others.

Buffalo certainly earned and deserved the name 'Gentle Giant' at the Sanctuary. He was dearly loved by our visitors and it was a very sad day when he died just after Christmas in 1987. He was forty years old.

Busby

Busby is a dark brown gelding with a white muzzle. He was born in 1990 and relinquished to The Donkey Sanctuary in 1993. His owners, who had bought him as a colt in a market, found that he wasn't getting along with their ponies so they reluctantly sent him into our care. As he grew up, Busby's gentle, quiet nature shone through and in 2001 he joined EST Sidmouth to work with children with special educational needs and disabilities. He is quite a small donkey and ideal to be with children who are nervous, as he is so calm and well-behaved. He stands so still as he's groomed by the children that he sometimes appears to have dozed off, but he also has his energetic moments – often galloping round and round his field to make sure he is the last to be caught when it's time to go back into the stable!

Busby has many visitors in his role as one of the donkeys in EST Sidmouth's Adoption Scheme.

Butch

When Butch came to the Sanctuary in 1988 our driver reported it was the saddest collection he had ever made. Jack, Butch's owner, was eighty years old and for the last twenty-five years they had been inseparable companions. Knowing he was no longer able to care for Butch as he grew older, Jack made the sad decision to send him to the Sanctuary. Having handed the driver a suitcase containing Butch's belongings, Jack was too upset to let the lorry go and for half an hour he sat inside with Butch's head on his shoulder. Even the driver had tears in his eyes as he finally had to close the tailgate and set off for Devon. However, for the next seven years Jack visited the Sanctuary three

ABOVE *Butch was an old softie*

Busby

or four times a year and would spend every day sitting in the Main Yard, with Butch never leaving him. Then, another tragedy: Jack died.

One day a few weeks later Butch was seen resting his head on the shoulder of an elderly visitor who was sitting on the same seat as Jack did when visiting! I felt so sorry for Butch, as he was obviously missing Jack, so we advertised in the local papers for a grey-haired gentleman to make regular visits to him. Butch enjoyed visits from the kind gentleman who volunteered, but the visits ended when the gentleman became ill. As a resident in Main Yard, though, he continued to receive lots of fuss and cuddles from our many visitors. I wasn't at all surprised, though, when one of our Donkey Week visitors told me that she had been sitting on the same bench when, as she said to me, 'this old donkey came and put his head on my shoulder – and kept me there for half an hour!' I didn't need to ask the name of the donkey, and when I told her the story of Butch and Jack she was visibly moved.

DONKEY FACTS, PEOPLE AND PLACES

Beach donkeys

Donkeys have been giving rides to children on UK beaches since Victorian times, but for many years I had been concerned with regard to the conditions under which they worked. I realised that many of them were unfit, overworked, underfed and expected to work long hours on beaches, carrying loads far too heavy for them. I was actually threatened on one beach for telling the operator off for working a mare that had just recently foaled. She was being prodded on by an electrically-operated goad, leaving her heartbroken foal on the edge of the beach.

Over the years conditions for the donkeys have been improving, thanks to our work with other equine charities and local councils – and with many beach operators' willing co-operation. Compiled with the co-operation of Blackpool Council and put into operation a few years ago, we have now updated The Donkey Sanctuary Code of Practice for Working Donkeys, which has been endorsed by the British Equine Veterinary Association. The first copy was presented to the Mayor of Blackpool, which has the largest number of donkeys in the UK working on its beaches.

Donkeys working on the beach at Rhyl in North Wales

Bonaire

I had been made aware of difficulties for donkeys on the Dutch island of Bonaire in the Caribbean, where feral donkeys were wandering onto the roads, causing accidents and being killed.

In 1993, while cruising in the Caribbean with my friend, June, one of the ship's ports of call was Bonaire and we took the opportunity to visit to see the problem for ourselves. We saw that the donkeys, many of them very thin, were wandering all over the roads as our taxi drove us to the site of a small Sanctuary, which was being run by a Dutch lady named Marina Melis.

The Sanctuary was small but very well run, and Marina appeared to be gaining control of the donkey situation. However, she was very grateful for our offer of help. We agreed that The Sanctuary would send a donation to build a second shelter, assist with fencing and, at a later date, provide collars for the donkeys.

The Donkey Sanctuary Bonaire has since expanded and we continue to help in a small way.

The donkey's bray

In the wild most braying is performed by territorial males. They tend to bray regularly soon after dawn and sometimes are answered by other males. The leaders of the herd bray to maintain contact with the group and advertise group possession of the area to other herds. They also bray before rounding up the group to move to a new location. Therefore it would seem that braying is a natural feature that has stayed with the donkey throughout the centuries.

Can you hear me?

Legend has it that after hiding in Egypt for some years Joseph decided to move his family back to Nazareth. During the night they camped along the side of the road and one night while they slept, their donkey heard the soldiers' horses approaching from a distance. Afraid that the soldiers were coming to kill Jesus, the donkey neighed to wake Joseph. He neighed and neighed, but his voice was just too soft to wake the sleepers. Finally, as the soldiers approached, the donkey prayed for a loud voice to wake the family. When he neighed again, he was rewarded with the loud bray that donkeys have had ever since.

DONKEYS

Charlie C

Charlie C is one of the donkeys giving rides to children with special educational needs and disabilities at the EST Centre in Sutton Park near Birmingham. He is a broken-coloured gelding and was born in 1992. His previous owners moved to Clovelly in North Devon when Charlie was three years old, and he was kept with the well-known Clovelly donkeys.

Clovelly is well known for its quaintness, its lovely harbour and for having a team of working donkeys. The main street dips steeply to the harbour, and is very narrow and cobbled. For many years the donkeys carried all sorts of goods up and down the narrow streets, including fish from the harbour, beer barrels and empty bottles and rubbish from the New Inn, laundry and visitors' luggage. Nowadays, though, they can be seen carrying children around their meadow at the top of the village or posing for photographs in the street.

When Charlie was very young he would follow the other donkeys when they were giving rides, even though he was not old enough to work. In 1996 Charlie's owner decided he could no longer keep him, so he was sent in to The Donkey Sanctuary. He spent a year at the Sidmouth Centre before moving to EST Birmingham. The staff at the Centre say he's a real star; not only is he ridden by the children, he also pulls the cart and, when needed, will travel to residential homes on the Centre's Outreach Programme. He is kind and gentle, and interested in everything! He loves the children and the children love him!

One of Charlie's best fans is a wonderful 100-year-old lady who visits him on a regular basis. When she leaves we have to wipe the lipstick marks from his nose where he has received so many kisses and cuddles!

Charlie C

Chloe

Chloe

Staff at the Cyprus Donkey Sanctuary collected Chloe in May 2007 from a small village in the Troodos Mountains after a villager had contacted us when he'd heard that Chloe's elderly owner was going to poison her. Chloe was only three years old at the time and the owner had found her too young and boisterous to handle and work. She had a very eventful journey back to the Sanctuary as one of the brakes on the horsebox seized up while coming down a steep road! Despite every effort by the driver, including hitting it with a hammer, the brake wouldn't budge. There were no houses or any other buildings in sight and the daylight was beginning to fade. Fortunately, the Sanctuary's maintenance man, Petros, drove for almost two hours to come to the rescue. Petros can fix almost anything but because the brake was stuck and couldn't be freed, the wheel wouldn't turn and so the only option was to take the wheel off! A very slow and careful journey on three wheels eventually ensued! Dear Chloe, who had never been in a horsebox in her life, seemed totally unfazed and was a paragon of virtue throughout the whole episode, arriving at Vouni as if she had done this sort of thing for years.

Chloe soon befriended one of our grooms who took care of her while she was in the isolation unit, and she was very upset when he was off work for a few weeks. All the female grooms at the Sanctuary are quite envious of her lovely blonde and reddish highlights, which stay in her coat all year round. She's a very friendly donkey and is ideal for her role as an 'adoption donkey'.

Christon

Christon

Christon was an unwanted young stallion who was taken into care at the Donkey Sanctuary (Cyprus) on 3rd July 2008. His owner had bought him six months earlier as a present for his small children but soon realised that there was a lot more to looking after a donkey than he first thought – and that a stallion wasn't the best type of donkey for young children to handle. As the owner didn't live near where the donkey was kept, a very kind neighbour took care of him until we could bring him to the Sanctuary.

As we have a non-breeding policy and stallions can be aggressive, it was necessary for Christon to be castrated before he could join new friends at the Sanctuary. The operation went very well and he was up on his feet in no time. An added bonus to the operation was that he calmed down very well afterwards!

Cisco

Cisco, a dark sorrel-coloured donkey, is one of the resident team of donkeys at EST Birmingham. He is a seven-year-old miniature, who was relinquished to The Donkey Sanctuary in 2008. He'd belonged to a breeder, who found that Cisco didn't seem to be performing his duties properly, so he was sent into our care.

Although he is the smallest donkey at the Centre he loves to play with the other donkeys. He runs around the field teasing them, until one of them decides to join him. This is usually a donkey named Rambo.

Cisco is being trained to go out on outreach work, visiting schools and residential homes. Bearing in mind how small he is, he will, no doubt, be very popular with everyone!

Cocoa

Cocoa is a handsome chocolate brown gelding, born in 1994. He came from a kind and loving home and had been shown and ridden before coming into The Donkey Sanctuary. Unfortunately for various reasons his owner could no longer keep him, so in 2002 he was relinquished to the Sanctuary.

Cocoa soon became very popular with the staff and, with his cheeky personality and easy-going nature, they thought he would make a perfect donkey to work with disadvantaged children. After some training he was transferred to the EST Manchester Centre and is now one of the most popular donkeys there. He is also one of the four donkeys in the Adoption Scheme.

Although Cocoa no longer takes part in the riding sessions, he still wants to be in the heart of everything that goes on, so takes his role as a 'cuddle and grooming' donkey very seriously. Cocoa loves it when the children choose him

Cisco, with his playmate, Rambo

Cocoa

to groom, standing quietly as they brush his soft coat and gaze in wonder at his panda-like eyes. Who could resist him?

Although his best friend is Soufflé, he's recently made friends with Tufty, the most mischievous donkey in the group. We hope he doesn't pick up any of Tufty's cheeky ways!

Crackers

In 1983 a concerned member of the public rang one of our Welfare Officers to say that, despite many enquiries, she and her husband had been unable to find the owner of a donkey wandering on waste ground at the side of her property. The donkey had, apparently, been wandering in and out of the traffic in town for six weeks or more and, despite requests to other sources, nothing had been done. We collected him the same day and found him far too ill to make the journey to Devon so he was taken to our Welfare Officer's home. A local veterinary surgeon was immediately called in and the full extent of the donkey's suffering became apparent. He was aged between two and three years, had bad anaemia, loud lung noises due to untreated pneumonia, a very bad wound on the hind leg which had turned septic, an eye injury which had not been treated and had caused the eye to mist, worm infestation and severe lice. Add to this the fact he'd had no proper food for six weeks and rainwater puddles as the only liquid, you can understand his distress.

As it was near Christmas we decided to name him Crackers, and for him it really was Christmas! Soothing ointment was smoothed on his painful leg with gentle caring hands and he was given a small feed of oats, flaked maize, bran and carrots to begin the gradual feed-up necessary to restore him to health.

The first few days with deep straw to lie on, ad lib hay and regular food must have been like heaven to him and he became strong enough to travel to Devon, where he settled down on the road to recovery amongst the 1,800 donkeys we had in our care at that time. I wonder how people could possibly be so cruel as to allow him to wander around in such a state.

Crackers was in a terrible state when he arrived in our care

DONKEY FACTS, PEOPLE AND PLACES

Candlelight Evenings

The Donkey Sanctuary becomes a magical place at its annual Candlelight Evenings, held in December, when a dazzling array of candles, each one representing the memory of a supporter's loved-one, light up the sky.

In 2009 over 15,000 candles were arranged by staff around the Sanctuary in various shapes and designs, mainly on a Christmas theme. The Reverend Peter Leverton and I led a special carol service, splendidly accompanied by the Ross-on-Wye Town Band, and over 2,000 visitors attended. For the first time the carol service was broadcast live on the internet, and over 1,700 people in forty-two countries were able to enjoy the event too.

The Donkey Sanctuary is a magical place on Candlelight Evenings

Cerys

When Cerys Edwards was horrifically injured in a car accident as a one-year-old the doctors advised the family that she would never walk, talk or breathe on her own. She had suffered multiple injuries, including complete paralysis and considerable brain damage.

Four years later, since the family became aware of the work of EST at the Birmingham Centre in 2009, they have been thrilled with the progress that she has made since she began attending sessions. Cerys' mother, Tracey, says:

'It's been lovely to see how much Cerys loves coming to her riding sessions. Her face lights up when she sees the donkeys. Our visits are not only fun but also provide many physical benefits, and there's been a noticeable improvement in her posture and head control since we started coming to EST. Her favourite donkey is Hugo because he is so friendly and she loves the way he trots! The staff are amazing; they understand and support the special needs that Cerys has. It's a breath of fresh air to come here each week because it's such a happy, safe environment.'

Cerys continues to make incredible progress and recently astonished doctors at Stoke Mandeville hospital by standing up for the first time with the aid of calipers and also breathing without the use of a ventilator for up to five minutes.

Cerys has made marvellous progress since she started attending the Birmingham EST Centre

Charlie

Charlie is profoundly autistic and struggles to communicate or interact socially, affecting his everyday life, but his anxieties are eased once a week when he rides donkeys at the Leeds Centre of the Elisabeth Svendsen Trust for Children and Donkeys.

His mother, Kirsty, home-educates Charlie and follows Son-Rise, an autism-specific programme. She also engages Charlie in a range of therapies that have been a great help in developing his abilities. One of these is donkey riding therapy, which has had one of the most positive impacts on Charlie's life. Kirsty first took Charlie for donkey-riding therapy at the Centre near Eccup in Leeds when he was three years old. She never thought she would see her son ride a donkey, but his progress was to prove more dramatic than anyone expected. Kirsty says:

> 'Charlie was just like any other young boy until he was two-and-a-half, when his autism caused him to regress from social interactions. He lost the speech and language that he had learned and avoided making eye contact. He would spend all day banging his head against the wall and he screamed throughout the night. It was just devastating.

When I first brought Charlie to the Centre, I was sceptical of how the donkeys could help him; he wouldn't get on a bike or anything like that and I just thought… he will never ride a donkey.

To begin with he would only ride in a cart being pulled by a donkey, but gradually over time, he became brave enough to stroke the donkeys, and later sit and ride on them. Now he takes part in every aspect of the riding session. He's made so much progress and it's very moving to see what he achieves as the weeks go by. I am amazed at his bravery when he gets on the donkey – not just sitting there but taking part in different games. I really didn't think it was possible, so it's been life-changing for us both. I've brought every member of my family to the Centre in recent months so that they can see how much Charlie has improved. They all watch with tears in their eyes!'

Charlie loves riding the donkeys at the EST Leeds Centre

China

China is a dynamic country going through rapid economic and social change. This is impacting on the donkey and mule population which, at nearly ten million, is the largest in the world. Working with the Chinese Agricultural University, The Donkey Sanctuary has been visiting China since 2006, pursuing a strategy to understand the problems faced by donkeys, mules and their owners, and the ways that these may be addressed. To understand the realities 'on the ground', during each visit every opportunity is taken to see as many working donkeys, commercial farms, markets and slaughterhouses as possible. We actively engage with owners, facility managers and service providers to discuss welfare issues and advocate for improvements. For service providers we have carried out workshops on donkey health and welfare in Gansu and Inner Mongolia, university lectures throughout China and one national conference in Beijing in 2008. By developing mutual understanding and exchanging information with all people involved with donkeys, as partners we hope to increase awareness of welfare issues at a local and national level, as well as provide practical professional support to owners and service providers.

A working donkey in China

Collecting donkey memorabilia

Silver

Donkeys have featured in art in all its forms for hundred of years. An early example is on the Bayeux Tapestry, which depicts the events leading up to the Norman conquest of England as well as the events of the invasion itself. There are two donkeys featured on the tapestry – one is ploughing and the other one is grazing.

My silver brooch

I have always been interested in antiques and for a long time have been an avid collector, particularly where donkeys are concerned. My small collection ranges from a tiny silver and pearl donkey brooch to some beautiful oil paintings. The brooch is a particular treasure of mine, but it is so fragile I hardly dare wear it. It's an excellent example of Victorian silver-smiths at their best.

More robust are the many silver donkeys, some just stand-ing or in repose, whereas some are quite large table ornaments. A delightful silver donkey inkwell was donated to The Donkey Sanctuary by a supporter, who has since unfortunately died. This lady was a regular visitor to 'Donkey Week'. I remember the lady running up to me on her first visit, saying breathlessly, 'Dr S, come quickly! There's a foal in the field that needs your help.' This cry has been heard many times, but happily it is often a donkey that is lying down in the sun and gone fast asleep, appearing dead to a concerned onlooker. In fact they can stay there for hours without even a twitch! But with a shout of his name, two big ears rise up and twitch – and all is well. In this case, however, the foal in question really did have a problem. A visitor had given him a whole carrot and he was choking. Holding his mouth open I could see

Silver donkey inkwell/pen stand

half of the carrot and, grasping the slimy edge firmly I was able to pull it out. We were both very relieved and the lady was delighted she had been able to help. She continued to attend 'Donkey Week' every year, and I was intrigued when, one year, she handed me a cardboard box, inside which, carefully wrapped in tissue paper was a beautiful silver donkey inkwell/pen stand. 'I want you to have this, Dr Svendsen,' she said. 'Not yet, though. You are to have it when I die, as long as you promise that it is placed in the centre of the table at every meeting of the Trustees, so that they never forget why they are here.' When she died a few years later, the donkey arrived, and the promise is being kept to this day – I passed it over to The Donkey Sanctuary when I retired as Chief Executive and he is brought out at every meeting!

Pottery

The Staffordshire area became a centre of pottery production in the seventeenth century due to the local availability of clay, salt, lead and coal. Many companies in what is now the Stoke-on-Trent area produced decorative figures. Their work really thrived in the nineteenth century. Many of the pieces they crafted illustrated life in England at the time and sometimes represented humorous versions of events. I was delighted to acquire this delightful pair

A pair of Staffordshire pottery working donkeys

Beswick donkey

of early donkeys, both working for their living in London; one at work delivering milk and the other carrying vegetables.

Throughout the twentieth century and even today porcelain manufacturers use donkeys as models. I am the proud owner of a handsome donkey, one of a series made by John Beswick Ltd. The family business ran from 1894 to 2002 and was well known for its Beatrix Potter collection. This donkey is all 'tacked up' and ready for riding!

Porcelain donkey – made in Spain by Lladró

Danish porcelain makers also used donkeys for many of their studies, and I particularly like the Lladró donkey, which was made in Spain. The pastel shades of pale blue, white and grey particularly caught my eye at an Antiques Fair.

Bronzes

Vienna bronzes originated in the middle of the nineteenth century and became world famous – so famous in fact that they were copied, and an association was formed similar to that of the silversmiths in the UK. A hallmark was produced to protect the genuine Vienna bronze. In 1860 Franz Bergman started a factory in Vienna, which his son, Franz Xavier Bergman took over in 1900. Bergman started to produce erotic figures and, instead of applying the name 'Bergman' to these, it was written backwards – so the word 'namgreb' appears on all the naughty bronzes! I have about six of them!

Vienna bronze manufacturers produced the most wonderful life-like figures, painted expertly and much sought-after. Unfortunately the donkey is not always shown in the best light! Whilst figures of lions were usually produced as proud and roaring, the donkey was often depicted as a figure of fun, such as having its tail pulled by a crocodile or, in the case of my bronze, being teased by monkeys.

A Vienna bronze

The Donkey Sanctuary and EST's bronze donkeys

In 1996 we were offered the opportunity to acquire a life-sized bronze sculpture of a donkey, which we felt would look lovely in our Memorial Garden. Ray Gonzalez, the sculptor, needed to base this on a perfectly-formed donkey – and Russell, son of Angelina and a member of EST Sidmouth's team was exactly that!

We were delighted with the sculpture and today it remains in place as a symbol of peace and tranquillity in what is now known as the Russell Garden. Many visitors to the Sanctuary enjoy coming along and including him in their photographs.

Ray also produced a series of smaller versions, and I bought the very first one of fifty which were made.

A few years later we were given the opportunity to have more full-sized donkey sculptures made. These now hold pride of place at our EST Centres in Birmingham, Leeds, Manchester and Ivybridge, and there is another one waiting in the wings for EST Belfast!

A smaller version of Russell, the bronze donkey in the Memorial Garden at The Donkey Sanctuary

Paintings

Donkeys have featured in pictures by many artists over the years and among my collection I have an early Victorian painting, artist unknown, which shows donkeys being ridden and misused for the entertainment of onlookers. Years ago people often poked fun at donkeys as well as misusing them. Donkey derbies were very popular and no one seemed to consider the welfare of the animals, which were ridden by adults, most of whom were too heavy. Today donkey derbies are much more regulated and controlled, and only children are allowed to ride.

A picture I found at an antique fair in Salisbury took my eye. It was by Arthur A Friedenson (1872–1955). He was ex-Royal Academy and had lived in Yorkshire, studying in Paris and Antwerp. I needed a really close look as it was difficult to see from a distance, so I had to ask the lady in charge if I could come behind her desk. We started talking and it transpired she was a great

Victorian painting showing donkeys being ridden and misused for the entertainment of onlookers

supporter of The Donkey Sanctuary and had recognised me from photographs in our newsletter. Even more of a coincidence, she was a relative of Arthur Friedenson and had obtained the picture from family as she loved the donkey featured. She didn't really want to sell it but very kindly allowed me to buy it, saying it couldn't be going to a better home!

Whilst modern paintings don't always catch my eye, I was interested in buying the painting of a beach scene by Robert Bailey (opposite page). Whilst the donkeys appear to be in good condition, the painting hangs in my office as a permanent reminder of the ongoing need for monitoring beach donkeys around the UK.

Approximately nine hundred donkeys work on our beaches every year and, on the whole, our requests for care of the donkeys are upheld nowadays. The Donkey Sanctuary has introduced an annual competition for the best kept beach donkey, which has ensured they have a much better deal than in the past. I personally have no objection to children of the correct weight riding donkeys. Many supporters when talking to me remember with pleasure their experiences as children with donkeys on the beach – often the highlight of their childhood holidays.

The Rainbow Donkey by Arthur Friedenson

Donkeys on the Beach by Robert Bailey

I have very fond memories of a kind and generous lady from the USA. During her visits to The Donkey Sanctuary Cordelia May became my friend, and she also became the donor of the largest gift The Donkey Sanctuary and EST have ever had.

One October day I was asked if I could see two American ladies who were visiting the Sanctuary. Mrs May was already a supporter and she and her companion, Betty Rahsman, loved donkeys, but this was the first time they'd come to see them. Once in my office I told them how the Sanctuary had begun and they were very upset to hear of the appalling condition some of the donkeys had arrived in. Then they asked if I could spare half an hour to show them some of the donkeys, which of course I did. As we walked past the car park I noticed their stretch limousine, complete with uniformed chauffeur. Cordelia told him they would be another half hour before they'd be ready for the return journey to London.

It was over two hours later when they returned to the car! Every donkey they saw had to be touched and patted! A recent intake who had just completed his isolation period was alone in paddock, separated from the group of donkeys he was about to join, but able to communicate with them through the fence. This two-year-old had been living alone in a dirty shack, abandoned by his owners, and was still afraid of humans despite his last two months at the Sanctuary. Cordelia, despite her eighty years, wanted to go and talk to him and, despite my concern, she was over the fence in a flash! To my delight the little donkey nuzzled her, and lapped up the fuss he was receiving. He and Cordelia obviously fell for each other! She remained in the paddock for a long time before regretfully climbing back over. I noticed the tears in her eyes as she returned to the car. As she left she gave me a donation of $1,000 and promised to return the following year.

She did – and the year after! She was due to visit again in the autumn of 2000 and on the appointed day I was working in my office when, all of a sudden, the door flew open and in walked Cordelia, Betty and their chauffeur, each of them carrying a parcel wrapped in brown paper. 'I've brought you a present, Dr S,' Cordelia said. 'I was walking through the Burlington Arcade in London and saw these – and I immediately thought of you!' The three of them started tearing off the brown paper to reveal three beautiful paintings! They are by the well-known artist William Weekes (1864–1904).

I broke down and cried. It was so unexpected and the paintings were lovely. I thanked her profusely and promised they would be kept by The Donkey Sanctuary for ever. They are still hanging in the Chief Executive's office to this day.

Cordelia's kindness didn't end there, though. As we sat talking, with the paintings propped up against my desk, she held my hand and asked, 'how are you off for money, dear?' I explained that both charities were struggling at the moment. She squeezed my hand and asked, 'would a million dollars help?' I couldn't believe my ears and the tears began to flow once more! True to her word, Cordelia arranged for her donation, which was divided into $750,000 for The Donkey Sanctuary and $250,000 for EST, to be sent to us through the American Charities Aid Foundation.

'Mother and foal'

What a wonderful lady! When she died a few years later, her trust fund paid for me to visit Pittsburgh to attend a commemoration service for her. It was an

'A family affair'

RIGHT *'Giving way'*

amazing ceremony with pictures of her with our donkeys everywhere. I will never forget Cordelia May!

Cyprus

- After financially assisting the Friends of the Cyprus Donkey since 2004 and following the retirement of the owners, The Donkey Sanctuary took over in 2007. The Donkey Sanctuary (Cyprus) was registered as a non-profit making organisation in Cyprus to continue caring for over 120 donkeys at the Sanctuary and helping other donkeys on the island.
- The Sanctuary is situated in Vouni in the Limassol District. It is open every day from 10am to 4pm and admission is free.
- Due to the limited space available and the terrain at Vouni, two holding bases were set up near to the Sanctuary – the first in 2009 and the second in 2010. Although not open to the public, both locations provide spacious accommodation on flat land and continue to provide the best standards of care for almost seventy donkeys.
- On average, one donkey is taken into care every month.
- Every donkey enjoys loving care provided by dedicated staff and volunteers, and receives regular health checks by the farrier and vet.
- Education to visiting schoolchildren is given throughout the year and, by prior arrangement, visitors can participate in grooming and donkey walking.
- Volunteers from other countries frequently come to stay at Vouni to work with the staff taking care of the donkeys and learning about what is involved.
- A Welfare Officer visits most of the zoos, trekking centres and other places that use donkeys as an attraction, to give advice and support.
- The Sanctuary provides advice to owners enabling them to take better care of their donkeys and increase their knowledge.
- An Outreach Programme is in place, visiting the districts of Larnaca, Limassol, Nicosia, Famagusta and Paphos providing free hoof care, dental treatments and anti-parasitic medication.
- Donkeys remain an important agricultural animal on the island, particularly working in the vineyards where machinery is not viable.

Feeding time in Cyprus!

DONKEYS

Danielle

In the late 1980s I was made aware of the plight of the Poitou donkeys in France. The breed was threatened with extinction and there were only sixty left in the world. Following discussions and meetings in France with Jacques Moreau, a leading expert on the breed and founder of SABAUD (Association pour la Sauvegarde du Baudet du Poitou) the unusual step was taken to allow The Donkey Sanctuary to take two of their mares, Jonquille and Amande, and a stallion (Torrent) out of the country to try to help conserve the breed.

Danielle towers above me!

Happily, Jonquille gave birth to a delightful filly foal in March 1991, who we named Danielle. She was the most unusual foal, already larger at birth than most foals are at three or four months, and with a dark brown curly coat. By the following year, Danielle had grown to almost twelve hands high – a rather large donkey as you can see from the photograph!

David

Occasionally donkeys are born with floppy ears, where the cartilage is not sufficiently hard to hold them up. Nineteen-year-old David was one such donkey. He came into the Sanctuary with no donkey social skills at all; as a stallion he'd spent a lot of his time on his own, only mixing with other donkeys when he was brought to cover mares. When he was retired to the Sanctuary it was almost as if he didn't know he was a donkey – he was very frightened of his new surroundings and the other donkeys close by, and would huddle in the corner of the barn. He was given his own private quarters and in due course had the necessary operation to enable us to introduce him slowly to a small group of donkeys for a few hours at a time. We had to teach him how to be a donkey!

You wouldn't believe it to see him now – he's a different chap and loves living in his male-only group where he plays and interacts with them like a normal donkey does. With his sunny and affectionate nature he's a real favourite with the staff, especially the girls (in fact the girls have posted a 'David Appreciation Group' on Facebook!). He's a star and he knows it!

Having worked at EST Sidmouth for sixteen years Daniel has now been retired to Shelter One with his ex-adoption colleagues, Tapestry and Tom Harrison. They all love the attention they receive from the Sanctuary's many visitors.

David looking for a cuddle!

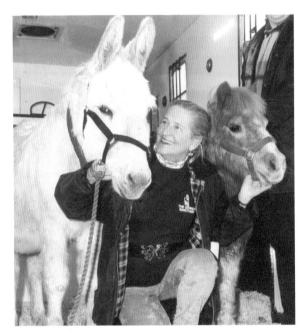

I met Dinky and Miner as they arrived at the Sanctuary

Dinky

In 1994 Dinky had the honour of arriving as our six thousandth admission. He must have been wondering what was happening as the lorry arrived, as there to greet him as he was led down the lorry ramp were press photographers, eagerly crowding around trying to get the best shot of this thirty-five-year-old celebrity!

At one stage of his life Dinky was a well-known character in Durham, where he visited the marketplace pulling a smart little trap. He was especially popular at Christmas! He was purchased in 1969, at the age of about ten, as a birthday present for a lady from her husband and he had a loving and happy home. However, the family decided to move to Saudia Arabia and, as they told us, 'we need to know he will be looked after properly in his old age'.

Dinky was quite a character. He was an expert escapologist, rolling under wire fences to visit other donkeys and even climbing up steep stairs in a barn to reach the new season's hay (it took four men to get him down!). When we found that Dinky had lived most of his life with 'Miner', a Shetland pony, we offered Miner a home as well.

Dolly

Dolly was born around 2002 and had been kept as a pet by a hotelier in the Paphos area of Cyprus. She had been known to the staff at The Donkey Sanctuary (Cyprus) for some time as, despite giving the owner lots of advice not to feed her large amounts of barley and bread, he continued to do so and she got very fat. Unfortunately, as with most donkeys, she would eat absolutely

Dolly

anything she could get hold of and, as a result of being so overweight, she developed a very painful hoof condition called laminitis. The Sanctuary's Welfare Officer, farrier and vet visited her several times to treat her for the problem, but eventually her owner asked us to take her into care, mainly due to lack of time to care for her and her hoof problems.

Dolly has to stick to a strict diet and have her feet trimmed regularly to try to prevent her getting further attacks of laminitis. Because of the previous laminitis, she has rather thin soles and if she treads on a big stone her feet can get a little bruised. She is an absolute sweetheart and will stand so patiently when she occasionally has to have a soft pad and bandage put on her hooves. Dolly also likes to be with the geldings in the paddock and can be quite a flirt! Maybe we should call her 'Dollybird'?

Donk Dean

Donk Dean came into our care in 1991 and works at the EST Birmingham Centre. He'd belonged to an elderly couple but had proved to be too much of a handful for them. He had been kept as a single donkey and obviously his boredom had resulted in naughtiness as, once he joined other donkeys at the Sanctuary he was no problem whatsoever!

Donk Dean

DONKEY FACTS, PEOPLE AND PLACES

Daniel

Daniel has autistic spectrum disorder. On his first visit to the Sidmouth EST Centre he was terrified of getting close to the donkeys and would only watch them from a distance. However, over time, and with the help of an older friend, he progressed to riding in the donkey cart – but he still wouldn't touch the donkeys. He would cling, screaming, to his teacher and refuse to look at them.

After several visits Daniel now enjoys riding every fortnight and even says 'thank you' to the donkeys by stroking them at the end of his ride. He's so much happier and more relaxed, and the staff are delighted at the wonderful progress he's made since he first came along. For his efforts he won the Charles Judge Memorial Cup for Courage, which was presented to him at the 2009 Summer Fair. He was so proud!

Daniel enjoying his donkey ride

The Derbyshire Centre

As part of The Donkey Sanctuary, the Derbyshire Centre (formerly known as Newton Farm) in Flagg, near Buxton, is currently home to forty donkeys taken into the charity's care. As well as the care of its resident donkeys, staff at the Centre hold regular training courses for donkey owners.

The Centre holds occasional Open Days for visitors to come along and see the work being carried out. Chris Pile, manager, says:

> 'Not many people know The Donkey Sanctuary has a base in the Peak District, simply because we're not normally open to the public. We provide permanent refuge to a small number of donkeys who are elderly or have long-term medical conditions, whilst other donkeys are provided with respite care until they are fit enough to travel to the main Sanctuary in Devon.'

To find out more visit www.thedonkeysanctuary.org.uk/derbyshire or call the Derbyshire Centre on (01298) 83866.

Donkeys at the Derbyshire Centre

Donkey Breed Society Junior Camps

Contributed by Maggie Taylor, Community Fundraising Assistant at The Donkey Sanctuary.

The Donkey Breed Society (DBS) is a British organisation and was founded in 1967. It seeks to encourage a fuller and more active life for those donkeys who are much loved family pets or companions to other animals, and has worked to achieve this on behalf of all donkeys since its inception.

The Junior Section is for all children, whether they are lucky enough to own donkeys or who simply love them and want to learn more about them. Members are given information, advice, training and activities, one being the camps held annually at The Donkey Sanctuary. The children are brought along to use the facilities of the EST Sidmouth Centre for a week during the school summer holidays and learn about donkey care and the work of The Donkey Sanctuary. Since the first camp, literally hundreds of DBS Juniors have been able to enjoy the beautiful and peaceful surroundings of The Donkey Sanctuary, and the love of donkeys has led several ex-campers to become vets or follow other careers with equines and other animals.

DBS Juniors at The Donkey Sanctuary's Training Centre

Donkey Week

Contributed by Maureen (Mo) Flenley, a long-term supporter

I first saw an advertisement for Donkey Week in a national newspaper twenty-seven years ago, and I decided that seeing donkeys would be an ideal holiday for me, especially as I had never been to Devon before. Sadly that first week was already fully booked, so I made sure of my place in May of the following year, and have been going ever since!

I enjoyed my first visit so much, and seeing those wonderful donkeys was marvellous. Mother (as she likes us to call her) turned out to be the most wonderful person I had ever met. She and her entire staff are so friendly and nothing seems to be too much trouble for us 'Donkey Weekers'. There are so many of us who attend year after year – some from overseas but mainly from all over the UK. I have made so many new friends from those very happy weeks – not only human – but donkeys too! Although a few special donkeys have passed away over the years, I still have some extra special friends at Slade House Farm, as well as two favourites at Brookfield Farm, named Cain and Cormac. I like to visit these special donkeys every May during Donkey Week, as well as in October at Memorial Day.

During Donkey Week coach trips are available so that we can also visit the other farms, where hundreds of other donkeys live and which are not normally open to the public. The staff arrange various events for the evenings, such as quiz nights and dances, which are optional but are so popular with everyone. Those Donkey Weekers who have attended for ten years or more are invited to a lunch in their honour and every new 'ten-yearer' is presented with a special red sweatshirt. The sweatshirt makes us feel experts in all things donkey-related and helps us pass on our knowledge and experience to any newcomers during the week!

Mention must also be made that admission to The Donkey Sanctuary is FREE, and there is a super restaurant, where meals, drinks and ice-creams are always available. A MUST is a visit to the Visitor Centre, which sells books, cards and numerous other souvenirs – all on a donkey theme, of course!

Mo with one of her favourites!

DONKEYS

Eeyore

Of all the foals that have been born at the Sanctuary I think Eeyore gave me the most joy. Despite her earlier ordeal Smartie (see her story under 'S') gave birth in 1974 to a very sturdy foal. He was the most beautiful shade of grey and even at birth the cross on his back was clearly marked.

Eeyore was such a little mischief! His poor mother only had to lie down in the field to rest and he would nudge her, push her and try, frequently and noisily, to jump right over her! It was a good job she was fully recovered, as he was into everything. I was frequently called by a desperate Smartie as Eeyore had got under the fence and was happily exploring pastures new, with Smartie helpless on the other side. When I tried to guide him back he would playfully kick his heels up and I really had to watch what he was doing – he could sometimes give me quite a hard, well-directed thump!

The farrier was the first to appreciate what a naughty donkey Eeyore could be. To do Smartie's hooves he would bend down with his back to her head and, grasping her hoof between his knees, clip away the excess horn and then file the hoof to the correct shape. It took a good deal of concentration and he tended to ignore the dear little foal nuzzling round him until – 'Ouch!' – the hoof was dropped and the farrier's hands clutched his bottom! Eeyore had found a new game which was much more fun than teasing his mother!

The Sanctuary was growing fast and Eeyore had a large number of new friends to play with. I think he enjoyed the move to Slade House Farm from the Salston Hotel more than anyone. Being led onto a lorry brings back real memories of terror to many donkeys and Smartie certainly felt fear and stopped, trembling, her feet on the ramp.

'It's all right, Smartie', I said. 'Only a few miles to a lovely new home', but she still hesitated. Then 'clatter, clatter, clatter', and past her trotted Eeyore – up the ramp to gaze down at his mother as if to ask, 'what on earth is the matter?' Smartie hesitated no longer and went up into the box; at this, just as the doors were closing, Eeyore shot past us all, down the ramp and out into the yard! Laughing, we went down and herded him up the ramp again. It seemed so easy – half way! Then with no effort at all he hunched himself up with all four little legs together, leapt over the side of the ramp and was off up the drive! Chasing after him we soon found that he had stopped, just out of sight, pretending to eat some roses from the neighbour's garden. As soon as we got near – off he moved again; it was like playing the childhood game 'black puddings' or 'grandmother's footsteps'! Using our 'superior' intelligence we eventually caught him and this time carried him right onto the lorry, to be greeted by his very tight-lipped mother, who had not been at all amused!

Slade Farm was heaven for Eeyore. At night he, Smartie and the rest of their group went into a large airy barn and I can remember sinking gratefully into bed on the first night knowing that all were safely shut up for the night. I was, however, to be further educated! Eeyore found a way to open the door! I had latched it firmly, but from the little teeth marks round the latch the next morning I realised what had happened. Sometime during that night, Eeyore had let himself out and Maud, a very elderly donkey, who had assumed a type of 'grandma' role, managed to follow him before the door swung shut again. Off trotted Eeyore determined to explore his new surroundings!

I was awakened by Smartie's desperate braying and realised who was missing. I had to shut the top of the stable door as well when I went to look for Eeyore and Maud, or a desperate Smartie would have launched herself over the top! I stood quietly by the track and listened. Yes – there in an area of woodland close by was the mournful sepulchral bray of Maud. Armed with a torch and accompanied by my son Clive, I followed the sound. I soon found a – by now – very grateful Eeyore and Maud lost in the woods, and led them home!

By the next morning Eeyore was apparently quite happy to graze peacefully, but I got a little angry when I found that the donkeys' water butt was empty. Herb Fry had been working with me for years and he assured me he had filled it that morning. We assumed the bung at the bottom must have come out. Herb refilled the butt and all was well until tea time when, once again, it was empty. This time we put the donkeys in the barn for the night after refilling it and the cool, clear water was still there in the morning. The next day, as I was idly leaning on the fence watching the donkeys enjoying their early morning roll I saw Eeyore leave the others and sidle up to the water butt. He didn't want a drink – oh no – he bent down and closed his little teeth around the bung and, bracing his little hooves, he pulled it out and stood in delight watching the water run between his legs and down the field!

Water had a fatal fascination for him. His group (the nursery group) used to go out with the 'oldies' in the paddock by the intensive care unit, where there was a lovely shallow duck pond with gently sloping edges. One day there was a shout from one of the staff and we rushed out to rescue Nellie, an elderly donkey, who had somehow got herself into the middle of the pond and couldn't get out. She seemed fine after her ordeal and not a bit concerned, and we thought little more of the incident until one afternoon a little later. I was in the office and through my window I could see the donkeys. This time Gertrude was by the side of the pond dosing quietly, with her ears twitching. Up came Eeyore. He was standing very close to Gertrude and seemed to be leaning on her. I sprang from my seat and flung the window open, shouting, 'EEYORE!' But it was too late. As though in slow motion, Gertrude tottered on the edge and then landed in the pond with a great splash! It took three of us to get her out. Eeyore was confined to stables for the rest of the day!

Naughty Eeyore!

Eeyore continued to cause havoc throughout his life, particularly amongst the visitors, who would suddenly find their hats (particularly ones with bobbles) had been removed from their heads or handbags snatched away, by a little grey 'innocent-looking' donkey! He was such a popular character, but one thing he wasn't good at – we tried to train him for the Slade Centre (now EST) to give rides to disadvantaged children but his sense of humour proved too great. He couldn't resist stealing the children's toys and galloping off with them!

Eyeore helped the charity enormously, though, as he gave me the idea of writing a children's book featuring his adventures – all the stories in the book were true (with just a little poetic licence!) and sales of the book raised a magnificent amount for the Sanctuary over the next few years! Sadly Eeyore developed severe liver disease and died in 1989 at the age of only sixteen years. He is buried in the Rose Garden at The Donkey Sanctuary.

Eeyore and Pooh

The Donkey Sanctuary has been home to thirty-three donkeys named Eeyore since the charity began its work! One of them is currently available for adoption at EST Ivybridge, along with his best friend, Pooh. Their previous owners loved them both very much and were reluctant to part with them but, with a very young family to care for they felt the donkeys would benefit from more attention. They were delighted when Eeyore and Pooh were chosen to work with children with special educational needs and disabilities.

Eeyore and Pooh are inseparable, but they also like playing with their other friends at the Centre. Old wellington boots are a 'must have' toy in their stable. Eeyore in particular loves throwing them at the other donkeys, playing tug, or chasing his friends with one firmly held in his mouth!

Another favourite pastime for Eeyore happens when sheep are in the adjoining field. He runs up and down on his side of the fence, while the sheep do the same on their side! Backwards and forwards they run, until they've tired themselves out. Pooh looks on in amazement!

Eeyore and Pooh

Ember

On the morning of Saturday 16th May 2009 we received a phone call from a vet in Cheriton Bishop asking for advice regarding a two-week-old miniature foal, Ember. She was seriously ill, suffering with diarrhoea, bilateral blindness, lethargy and she was very dehydrated.

Elena, our vet on duty for the weekend, discussed the treatment and possible causes of Ember's symptoms over the phone but the vet was very concerned as the owners had lost two foals the previous year with similar symptoms. We therefore decided to hospitalise Ember and her mum immediately. Both were with us within half an hour and we started treatment after performing a head X-ray and an eye scan to try to determine the cause of the blindness. When our vets examined the eyes, they did not respond to the light and Ember had no vision.

Our veterinary team started treatment as soon as possible; antibiotics were given intravenously as well as anti-inflammatory drugs, anti-ulcer medication and fluid therapy. She also had to be fed through a tube as there were concerns about her not suckling enough from her mother. Other tests were carried out and blood and dung samples were taken to establish the cause of the illness. Two members of the team monitored her overnight, trying to keep her warm and comfortable and making sure she was suckling. The next morning she seemed much brighter. She was monitored and treated during the next twenty-four hours and by Monday morning she started to recover some sight and had no signs of diarrhoea.

Ember's results came back as rotavirus positive. Rotavirus is the most common form of infectious diarrhoea in foals. It is highly contagious and it can be easily spread by owners and staff and it is thought this was the cause of the loss of the two previous foals belonging to Ember's owners. Blindness can be seen in some foals when there is septicaemia present and this was the cause of Ember's blindness which, with the appropriate treatment, can be restored in some cases.

Thanks to our veterinary team we were able to save Ember and provide expert advice to the owners to prevent any foals contracting rotavirus in the future.

BELOW *Ten-year-old Erica was rescued from a meat market in the city of Leon in Northern Spain in 2003 by an animal welfare organisation called Animals Angels. She was about to be sold for slaughter, although she was in foal at the time. She was taken into care at our Spanish Sanctuary, El Refugio del Burrito, where she gave birth to her foal, who was named James.*

Ember with Vicky, one of our grooms at the hospital

Esmerelda

Esmerelda (see photo overleaf) was, for a long time, the oldest donkey at The Donkey Sanctuary. However, she died in December 2009 at the ripe of old age of fifty-six! She came into care with her son, Perseus, in 1993, her previous owners having reluctantly decided they hadn't the funds to care for them adequately. Perseus, himself a good age at thirty-four years, died in April 2010.

Esmerelda

Estrella

Estrella

Estrella is thirteen years old. She used to be kept as a pet by a couple in Granada but, unfortunately they had to move from their home. They didn't want to sell Estrella and were looking for a nice place for her to stay when they heard about El Refugio del Burrito, and they brought her to the Sanctuary themselves. She is now part of the Donkey Assisted Therapy for Children with Special Needs programme based at El Refugio. Being in a very good condition and such a gentle donkey, she was considered to be ideal for this activity. She thoroughly enjoys visiting children with special needs and disabilities at their schools; the work is very rewarding both for Estrella and all the children who enjoy her company.

Estrella and her best friend, Buenvenida, are regularly taken to meet children with special needs and elderly people in the Málaga area of Spain, and in March 2010 they were in Alhaurin de la Torre visiting the Early Care Centre and the Day Centre for the Elderly. They were accompanied by a television crew from Canal Sur's Salud al Día and were filmed as they worked.

DONKEY FACTS, PEOPLE AND PLACES

Education and Activities

The Donkey Sanctuary's Education and Activities unit has a team of dedicated donkeys and trained staff who provide interesting and educational activities for schoolchildren. Half-day or full-day on-site visits to The Donkey Sanctuary are available, where children can enjoy 'hands-on' interactive donkey education sessions as well as a guided tour of the Sanctuary and the opportunity to take part in a guided nature trail walk and Nature Centre activities.

School holiday activity sessions for schools and other children/youth groups (such as Brownies, Cubs, Guides, Scouts, Youth Clubs, Church groups etc.) are also offered. The unit also hosts events such as Life Skills and Activity Days, which include treasure hunts, a grooming session with the donkeys and team building.

In addition to providing these facilities at The Donkey Sanctuary, the E & A unit takes donkeys to schools around Devon, Cornwall, Somerset and Dorset. The school visits are educational, unique, interesting, interactive and exciting. The visits are attended by qualified staff, and include a thirty- minute interactive session involving grooming and donkey walking, giving children (as well as their teachers!) first hand experience of donkeys. The visits can be curriculum-linked on request.

Four donkeys are usually taken along, depending on pupil numbers. Leaflets and information packs for teachers are given to the teachers, and Donkey Sanctuary stickers are handed out to the children. Each class receives a certificate to say that the children have 'brushed, walked and learned about donkeys'.

Children enjoying an activity day

Edward

Five-year-old Edward has selective mutism, a rare disorder in which children will not speak in certain situations. In his case, it was first noticed when he was aged two. As he has two older siblings his father hadn't been concerned, as he thought it was normal that they did all the talking on Edward's behalf. However, the health visitor felt he should see a speech therapist. It was discovered that Edward had glue ear, which can lead to impaired hearing if left untreated. It was believed that, once this problem was addressed by inserting a grommet in his ear Edward's speech would improve. Unfortunately this was not the case and, as he was due to start school in September 2008, he was assigned a special needs co-ordinator to assess him before term began. She suggested that he might benefit from the unique donkey-riding therapy at EST Leeds.

Edward's father, Paul, explains, 'Edward will talk quite happily at home but, if we go out to the shops or somewhere we haven't been before, or even at school, he will not say a single word. Fortunately, since riding the donkeys he has opened up and will now speak confidently to members of staff there and will ask his donkey to 'walk on'. Kirsty Christmas, a riding instructor for the charity, says:

> 'Edward is a completely different child from when he first started his riding therapy a year ago. He chose not to communicate verbally and would only nod or shake his head in answer to questions. We first noticed him whispering commands into the donkey's ears during one of our riding sessions. He's now become a capable rider and enjoys playing

the games in the riding area. It's great to know that our donkeys have helped him so that everyone can hear him speak.'

Paul says that Edward now talks to his friends in the school playground and answers his teachers' questions. He talks about the donkeys a great deal, especially his favourite, Eeyore. He is so grateful that the donkeys have helped him so much.

Edward loves his contact with the donkeys

Egypt – our work there

I first visited Egypt in 1987, and had a good veterinary contact there in Dr Mourad Ragheb, who had previously attended one of The Donkey Sanctuary's special training courses. A twelve-month anthelmintic trial was set up within a sixty mile radius of Cairo, which I hoped would be the start of a larger project in Egypt, a country where donkeys and mules were in tremendous need of help.

However, it wasn't until 1992 that the first mobile clinic began operating, initially working in more than fifteen villages in Greater Cairo and in Matrouh in the north-west and expanding over the next two years with a second mobile clinic and visiting further villages.

Unfortunately, in 1995, due to the privatisation of the Egyptian veterinary services, The Donkey Sanctuary found it impossible to continue working in Egypt – but not before handing over its mobile clinics to The Brooke (formerly known as The Brooke Hospital for Animals) in Cairo so that the 'donkey work' could continue.

However, in the late 1990s The Donkey Sanctuary decided to help establish and fund a donkey welfare society in Egypt, and by March 2002 the Society for the Protection and Welfare of Donkeys and Mules in Egypt (SPWDME) was up and running. Having started with just one mobile clinic, run by the current project leader, Mourad Ragheb, and two other people, it now has three vets, an education officer, a harness maker and a farrier. They are supported by a team of animal health assistants who also carry out veterinary and farriery treatment and help improve harness, under the supervision of their team leaders.

The Donkey Sanctuary/SPWDME project initially concentrated on the poor farming communities near to Cairo in the Nile Delta, but began visiting brick kilns regularly in 2005, in an area called El Saf, south of Cairo. There are about 350 kilns in this area and of these we currently visit forty. This includes some that we started work with in 2009, some that we have been going to regularly for several years, and others which we have been asked to visit by owners who are aware of the work we are doing. Donkeys are used to pull heavy cartloads of bricks to and from the firing ovens. As well as providing veterinary and farriery treatments and advice, the teams supply good harness and show workers how to fit and maintain it, and our harness maker also trains local saddlers. Our education officer conducts sessions with both children and adult workers, increasing their empathy with their donkeys and teaching them how to care for them.

I had the opportunity to assist with treatment at a market in Egypt again in 2005

The teams also visit eleven villages around Cairo in the Nile Delta, some of which also have schools or agricultural colleges. A village visit will involve a mobile unit with vet, harness maker and education officer. Vets treat donkeys and give advice, the harness maker makes or adapts harness and gives advice, and the education officer talks to children in the village as well as giving donkey welfare lessons in the schools.

Shabaan, one of our vets, treating Soad, a donkey in Egypt

Donkeys in the brick kilns

There is some evidence that donkey welfare messages given through veterinary, education and harness work in the brick kilns in Egypt are being taken on board. As well as recognising that stronger, fitter donkeys work more effectively, some owners seem to have a generally caring attitude, and they run their kilns with the donkeys' welfare in mind.

One such case was found when the team visited a new kiln called Elhoria 2010. Vet Shaaban Fayez reported that there were nine donkeys working there, with a good body condition and no wounds from beating or poor harness. Food and clean water were available to them all the time and their stabling included an external yard which the owner, Khaled, had built himself.

Khaled told Shaaban he had worked in brick kilns for many years and decided to build his own seven months' previously. There was evidence of his concern for the donkeys in the design of the kiln, the care of the harness and carts, and the staffing arrangements. Shaaban says:

'All workers including the foreman and stockman are constant and are not changed, Khaled pays extra money to avoid them leaving the kiln, because he thinks the continuous change of workers has a bad effect on the donkeys. He says the working conditions at kilns are so hard for children, and they beat the donkeys, so he decided to bring in adults to work with them. They do not beat the donkeys. There are, therefore, no children working at the kiln, even though he pays more money for the adults.'

In addition, the donkeys only had to travel a short distance with the brick carts between the 'green' bricks and the furnace. Harness was changed regularly and the carts were also well-maintained. Lucky donkeys!

Unlike the brick kilns described in this story, in some kilns the donkeys still lead miserable lives

Yehia and Toto

The Donkey Sanctuary operates mobile units that visit rural communities in Egypt, providing donkeys with veterinary treatments and training owners on how best to care for their animals. On one visit, the team were delighted to see how eleven-year-old Yehia had learned how to make his own working donkey's halter as a result of demonstrations from the charity's harness maker, Farid.

Farid's sessions focus on teaching communities how to make harnesses that fit well and don't cause the wounds that are typically seen on working donkeys. The team sources materials that are easily and cheaply available in each particular region and then teaches communities to make harnesses from these materials so that they are able to replicate the good practices that they have been taught.

When Yehia visited the mobile unit in April 2010 to obtain treatments for fly bites to his donkey's legs, it was wonderful to see the quality of the harness that he had made for his donkey, Toto. Yehia had come up with the innovative idea of using reinforced strips of edging material from sacks along with the metal rings that are used for sealing the sacks.

With Toto's fly bites treated by vets at the clinic, Yehia was able to lead his donkey back home, where he encourages other donkey owners to take good care of the animals that contribute so much to their lives.

Yehia with his donkey

Ragab's donkey

In the photograph is one owner who impressed the team in Abo Ghaleb, a village near Cairo in the Nile Delta. Ragab Abdel El Hafez brought along his three-year-old female donkey which had been having treatment for lameness. The farrier made special shoes which cured the problem and Ragab had made 'socks' for the donkey's two front legs to protect them from flies and infection. The donkey also had dermatitis, so Ragab had trimmed her hair and treated it with henna. The halter was good and the nose-chain had been covered with cloth to avoid wounding.

Ragab with his donkey

The Elisabeth Svendsen Trust for Children and Donkeys (EST)

Contributed by John Akers, Chief Executive of EST

EST is a charity which makes provision for children with special educational needs and disabilities at purpose-built Centres located around the country. The children who attend have a wide range of disabilities. Some have learning difficulties; others are physically disadvantaged or have behavioural problems, brain damage or sensory impairment. EST aims to bring enjoyment and pleasure into the children's lives. In addition, in many cases our work helps with coordination, overall development, self-confidence, mobility, speech and language issues and self-esteem. Approximately 150 children a week attend each of our present six Centres. They are based at Sidmouth, Birmingham, Leeds, Manchester and Ivybridge (near Plymouth) and, more recently, Belfast. We were fortunate to receive most of the land for our newest Centre by way of a donation.

The children who attend can take part in riding sessions and they can also interact with the donkeys. Each Centre has driving carts and also sensory rooms for those children with sensory difficulties. They also have 'disabled-friendly' play facilities and equipment.

Starting lessons in the arena

The charity has made provision for many thousands of children with special needs and disabilities. It makes no charge to schools, parents/carers or the children. It very much relies on public subscription for operational funds.

EST does not solely work with children. Each of the Centres also has an 'Outreach programme', where visits are undertaken to local residential homes, nursing homes and hospices. The residents are greatly cheered by visits from the donkeys that are happy to climb up and down stairs!

EST is fortunate to have the support of two well-known figures in the equestrian world. The first is Mary King. Mary is a Trustee and renowned equestrian sportswoman. Among her achievements she has represented Great Britain at the Olympic Games on five occasions from 1992 to 2008 (winning one silver and one bronze medal). Our Patron is Lee Pearson. He has won nine gold medals for dressage in the Paralympics, as well as five World Championships and six European titles. He is an inspiration to us all.

The work of the charity is perhaps best illustrated by some individual examples, which you will find throughout this book.

The Ride

I just can't move my arms and legs
I really don't know why.
My Mum keeps saying 'please stand up'
And I do my best to try.

The days seem long, and I get tired
Lying on a bed all day
'If only something nice could happen'
I close my eyes and pray.

For seven long years I've been like this
Though my mind is really clear.
I can't understand why my legs won't work
And the adults say 'Never mind dear'.

But something happened yesterday
That has brought some hope to me
They lifted me into the family car
And they drove to a place near the sea.

And they wheeled my bed through a great big door
And they gave me a terrible fright.
Because in came an animal, oh so big
Who stood by me, and blocked out the light.

He put down his head and touched my hand
His breath was all warm and wet.
I could feel his soft hair brushing my arm
It was a feeling I'd come to forget.

And I longed to reach out and touch the long ears
And I longed to get out of my bed.
It was joy that I felt, as they lifted me up
And then put a hard hat on my head.

And then, oh – the thrill, I was up on his back
Looking down on my Mum and my Dad.
But why was she crying, and holding my hand
When I was feeling so glad?

The tingle I felt in my arm had come back –
I could feel a strange buzz in my feet.
And I tried and I tried to sit up straight
On my wonderful donkey so sweet.

But then it was over and back on the ground
They held me as close as they could.
For I longed and I prayed I could touch his soft nose
And my hands knew that they really should.

And he nuzzled my hand, and my fingers uncurled
And my arm moved the very first time.
And my tears wet his face as I knew that at last
With his help, God had given a sign.

Taken from Not Just Donkeys
by Dr Elisabeth D Svendsen and reproduced by
kind permission of Whittet Books Ltd

Adam is having a lovely time!

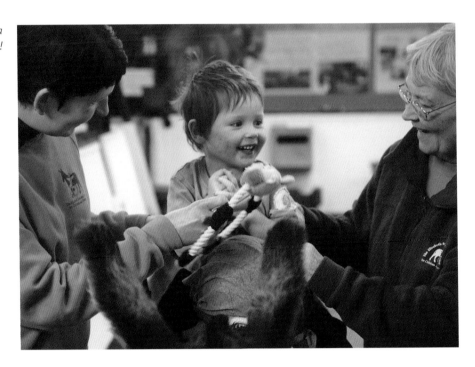

Something really special!

EST is something really very special. Where in the UK – or the world at that matter – could you find anything that even comes close to matching the concept and work of the Centres.

We, the 'family Hall', have a vested interest in promoting this side of the work and trying to enlighten the 'non-believers'. Sarah is very good at this. We became involved with donkeys in 1976, when we bought Cindy, a seven-year-old donkey, as a birthday present for Sarah. To say that we were 'green' on donkey matters was putting it mildly. It seemed a good idea at the time, but we needed all the help and advice we could get!

Not long after this Sarah started to go to an evening social club run by the Children's Society for children and young adults with learning difficulties. One of the voluntary helpers, Vic, soon got to know all about our donkey (Sarah is such a chatterbox!). While visiting his relatives he was able to visit The Donkey Sanctuary. He enjoyed himself so much that he urged us to go – which we did a year later. We found out about Donkey Week and the EST Centre and from that day on we were hooked!

Extract of letter received from Phil, Penny and Sarah Hall. Sarah is a volunteer at EST Birmingham. Phil and Penny help out at events held at the Centre and at Shows.

Sarah with her foster donkeys, Toffee and Penn, who were retired from EST Birmingham to live with the Hall family

Ethiopia – our work there

In 1986 I received an official invitation to visit Ethiopia from the University of Addis Ababa's Faculty of Veterinary Medicine, located in Debre Zeit, about forty kilometres from the city. My friend, June, and I were given a marvellous welcome by the Dean, Professor Feseha Gebreab, who showed us around the university buildings, including the operating theatre with its 'state of the art' equipment, which had been donated by other countries. Unfortunately this was all inoperable, as there was no electricity supply in that part of Debre Zeit at the time!

I will never forget my first visit to an Ethiopian market. It wasn't just the donkeys that were in an appalling condition; it was the number of women and children dressed almost completely in rags, crouched on the muddy ground trying to sell perhaps four pats of donkey dung, which had been dried out and to which a little straw had been added. This they were trying to sell as fuel. They would perhaps get one Ethiopian birr for it and, as a loaf of bread would cost three birrs, I realised the pitiful level of their existence. The donkeys were emaciated and had the most terrible wounds, and it occurred to me that the people had never been able to afford a doctor, let alone the luxury of a vet.

The Dean and I discussed the best way to help the donkeys in Ethiopia and it was agreed that The Donkey Sanctuary would provide funding for a joint project with the university.

The first mobile clinic began visiting the surrounding area in 1994, and in 1999 a new donkey clinic was built in the grounds of the Faculty compound providing an operating theatre, laboratory and training facility. Since then the Ethiopian operation has expanded into the Amhara region in the north-west of Ethiopia, the Tigray region in the far north, and SNNPRS (the Southern Nations, Nationalities and Peoples' Regional State) to the south. At Debre Zeit we now have thirteen front-line animal welfare staff: three vets, four animal health assistants and one animal attendant, three harness makers and two education officers. We have an additional clinic at Merkato (a large market in Addis Ababa). In each of the other three regions we have a vet who leads the team, supported by one or more animal health assistants who can also make and adapt pack saddles. Each regional base also has an education officer. These teams are based in the regional capitals of Bahir Dar (Amhara), Mek'ele (Tigray) and Hawassa (SNNPRS). The work takes staff to many different locations including markets, watering-points, vet clinics, schools and farmers' training centres; the team members who visit will vary according to the combination of vet/education/harness work needed.

Since wounds caused by inadequate pack saddles are a massive donkey welfare problem in Ethiopia, much of our work involves working with owners to demonstrate the benefits of better saddles and then ensuring that they can produce or access a sustainable supply. In several villages near our base at Debre Zeit we gave out free saddles to demonstrate their benefits and create a demand for them, and then trained local residents, including a group of women who needed employment, to make them. The locations were chosen because they all hold regular markets, attracting many donkey owners from the surrounding area, who would be likely to buy the saddles. In other regions we are training local saddlers to produce them, as well as sending our own harness-makers out with our mobile units to teach the technique to donkey owners or help them adapt their own pack saddles. We are monitoring our different approaches to assess which will prove most effective in the long run.

Vets and their fellow team members visit some sites regularly, such as watering points, markets, government vet clinics and the smaller animal health posts. Any treatment session is also seen as an opportunity to advise owners on how to prevent further problems, and help with the fitting or padding of the donkeys' pack saddles. Sometimes the harness-maker will adapt saddles or demonstrate how to make better ones. Visits to vet clinics and animal health posts are also a chance to improve the knowledge of the government vets and animal health workers, as they watch how we treat donkeys. We also give them more structured training.

School education is a big part of the Ethiopian teams' work. Education officers conduct sessions in schools on the care and needs of donkeys, their relationship with humans, and good/bad treatment. They also organise after-school donkey clubs with creative activities for pupils (producing stories, dramas, and poems) and practical ones (providing water for donkeys at nearby market sites). We are finding, in line with experience from other development

One of our vets, Tesfaye, working with a donkey owner

organisations that work with children complements our work with adults very effectively, and brings immediate benefits to donkeys.

In some of the rural areas around Debre Zeit work is underway to try and make donkey mistreatment and neglect socially unacceptable by using the influence of the leaders of Ethiopia's smallest administrative unit, the kebele. Community leaders could also make good donkey care a membership condition of some highly-respected neighbourhood associations and insurance schemes. The team have also been putting out donkey welfare messages at established community networking events in the villages, such as coffee ceremonies.

Donkey cart code of conduct

Our team in Hawassa, in the Southern Nations, Nationalities and Peoples' Regional State (SNNPRS), has been recognised for its work reducing road accidents involving donkey carts. The problem was raised during a workshop held in Hawassa at the end of December 2009, where The Donkey Sanctuary explained the aims of its programme there to a group of local delegates. These included people from the district agriculture and rural development offices, education, finance and economic development offices, the road transport authority and the Municipality. The road transport authority delegate raised his concern that while a large number of donkey carts travel by night, very few have plates or reflectors and the rest are almost invisible to car drivers. There was a high rate of accidents in which donkeys had been killed and vehicles damaged; people had also been injured and in some cases even killed. He described the situation as a 'real catastrophe' and said no government or NGO body was currently dealing with it.

The Donkey Sanctuary team agreed to take action and began working with the training and enforcement units of the local road transport authority, which does not licence vehicles but is responsible for controlling all road users including pedestrians, and ensuring that all vehicles are roadworthy. Our staff were able to advise on a code of conduct which the donkey cart drivers should be observing. As a result of this, the traffic police who enforce road safety laws began targeting donkey cart drivers who drive irresponsibly. While they cannot penalise drivers for donkey welfare 'offences' which do not compromise road safety, they now treat overloading and beating as safety offences (an overloaded cart may be less easy to control, and beating a donkey may cause it to veer into traffic).

To help make the carts more visible at night, the Hawassa team also designed and produced reflective plates carrying The Donkey Sanctuary logo. There were some initial problems with distribution and also how to affix the plates to the carts, but by June that year, sixty-five donkey carts had been fitted with a set of these reflectors and the owners had also been trained in how to balance loads on the cart better and prevent harness wounds.

To support the work we were doing, the road transport authority also introduced a trial system of ID cards and badges for donkey cart drivers. This was partly designed to tackle the problem of irresponsible under-age drivers – the minimum age is sixteen and those who were younger would not be eligible to register under this system.

In May 2010, on World Traffic Day, the Zonal Transport and Road Authority awarded a certificate of appreciation to the project team in Hawassa for all the work they have done to improve road safety. At the time of writing, the team were continuing to work with the Municipality to try and get the vehicle licence system extended to donkey carts.

The reflective plates are very effective

Mulu

A female donkey named Mulu had been unable to reproduce because of old injuries to her hindquarters. However, she is now a mother, thanks to surgery carried out by our Project Team Leader in Tigray, Dr Hagos Yhidego.

Mulu is an eight-year-old mare, owned by farmer Desu Redda and his family in the Hintalo Wajirat district of Ethiopia. She had been bitten by a hyena four years previously and the attack had left her with permanent damage, preventing her from mating. Two years ago she was brought to The Donkey Sanctuary's mobile clinic, where Dr Hagos carried out a surgical correction, which enabled Mulu to mate, conceive and give birth to a colt foal in December 2009. She has also mated successfully for a second time and the family expect her to produce further foals. 'The owner is very happy and brought her to the mobile clinic again, with her beloved foal,' said Dr Hagos. 'The success of the operation has become well-known locally and is serving to promote The Donkey Sanctuary's reputation.'

Mulu with her foal and her happy owner!

DONKEYS

Fergal and Angus

These four-year-old miniature donkeys were sent into our care in June 2009 by the well-known author, Frederick Forsyth, and his wife, Sandy. In Mr Forsyth's own words, 'Sandy and I are delighted that our two mischief makers, who were a bit too robust for us to deal with, are doing well and creating admirers. We continue to hold a great affection for them both.'

On arrival the two donkeys were rather nervous and didn't like being caught, but they soon got used to it and became more confident. They are strongly bonded to each other and are always found together. They love to play, and their groom can confirm that although they are real 'sweeties', they can be very mischievous. They are often the ringleaders of the group, encouraging all the other donkeys to gallop endlessly around the field. A favourite trick is to pull each other's collars off at every opportunity!

Fergal and Angus are currently in training to join our foster scheme, but sometimes they attend local and county shows, where everyone loves meeting these adorable little donkeys.

Fergal and Angus with our General Farm Manager, Annie Brown

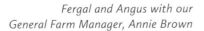

Flash

Flash was fifty-seven when he died in 2001, and even today he remains the holder of the record for being the oldest donkey at The Donkey Sanctuary. He was already an old man of forty when he arrived, and he spent most of his later years enjoying life to the full with a small group of friends on peaceful Paccombe Farm.

Flash with his friend, Arkle

Flynn

Flynn was purchased by his owner at a market in the north of England in 2000. His new home was a large field with other horses and ponies as companions. Unfortunately his new owner didn't have much experience with donkeys and for several years he was allowed to eat as much grass as he wanted. Eventually his feet began to suffer and he started to suffer from laminitis, a painful foot condition caused by congestion of the sensitive structures (laminae) within the foot. It became extremely difficult for him to walk and he developed a way to move around on his sore feet – by putting all his weight on his back legs and hopping around. Over time this affected Flynn's whole body. His shoulders changed shape, becoming over-developed by having to pull his painful feet around, and he started to develop a permanently arched back.

One day a member of the public saw Flynn's condition and contacted The Donkey Sanctuary. A Welfare Officer went to see him and recognised the signs of chronic pain that he was suffering. A few words with his owner made her realise that Flynn needed urgent veterinary care and he was signed over to the Sanctuary on the understanding that all efforts would be made to give him the best possible quality of life.

Flynn arrived at the Derbyshire Centre in Buxton in November 2007 and one of the vets from a local practice, Leire Ruiz de Alegria, was called out to see him. Seeing him with a deformed back and barely able to walk, Leire's first reaction was that he should be put down. But Chris Pile, the farm manager, persuaded her that he deserved a chance of life.

X-rays taken revealed that Flynn's pedal bones were damaged; a lot of the bone had literally disappeared with years of chronic pain, and he was left with hard stumps instead of well-formed bone. Darren Slater, the Centre's farrier, used the X-rays to work out a way of making Flynn's feet more comfortable and he built a set of plastic temporary foot supports which could be bandaged on his feet on a daily basis. Flynn was then able to hobble around his stable; he began to brighten up a little and bray to the other donkeys. A couple of weeks later Anne Sweeney, an equine physiotherapist began work on Flynn to relieve the muscular spasm in his back. Next, Mark Tabachnik, an equine vet, dealt with Flynn's neglected mouth. Flynn had overgrown teeth, with several sharp enamel points cutting into his gums and causing ulcers. At least now he would be able to eat in comfort.

Unfortunately it appeared that all this attention became too much for Flynn. He was used to living in a field with little or no human contact. He became very stressed and stopped eating. He'd been enjoying going to the gate of his yard to see the other donkeys – he even had a little rubber mat at the gate so he didn't have to stand on hard ground – but all he wanted to do now was lie down. Not even ginger biscuits could tempt him to eat.

A blood sample revealed he was suffering from hyperlipaemia, a condition often triggered by stress. Donkeys and small ponies are particularly susceptible

Flynn, wearing his warm rug

to this; it carries a high risk of fatality even when recognised promptly. When a donkey stops eating, the body tries to use the energy that is stored as fat deposits. As a result, free fatty acids are circulated to the liver to be converted to glucose for use by the body. This system is controlled by complex hormonal events. The large fat molecules in the bloodstream have consequences. If the energy source is not replaced and the process continues, the liver and kidneys will eventually block up and fail. Urgent treatment was required. Saline was administered intravenously to dilute the fats in Flynn's bloodstream, he was given multivitamins to help his liver function and he had daily insulin injections to stimulate his metabolism.

Leire and Mark visited Flynn daily, giving him valuable nutrition and fluids and, after a week of intensive treatment, on Christmas Eve 2007 he slowly started to eat again. A few weeks later he had recovered sufficiently to be put into a small field with a shelter. He continues to live happily at the Derbyshire Centre, where he will stay for the rest of his natural life.

Reproduced with the kind permission of Leire Ruiz de Alegria and Horse Magazine

Francesca with proud mum, Rosie

Francesca

On 2nd October 2008 a donkey named Rosie, who was in foal when she came into The Donkey Sanctuary's care the previous April, gave birth to the most delightful filly foal. She was a gorgeous soft bundle of brown and white fluff. I named her Francesca, as she was born two days before the Feast Day of St Francis of Assisi, the Patron Saint of Animals. A few hours after she was born, she was struggling to get to her feet, legs going in all directions. As soon as she could stand, Rosie gave her little nudges to guide her to where the milk was! Instinct tells a foal that the supply is underneath its mother somewhere, but they waste a lot of time looking under the front legs – and it's even more difficult if the foal keeps falling over! However, she soon sorted things out, and it was a great relief when she started suckling, getting the essential colostrum in her first feed.

DONKEY FACTS, PEOPLE AND PLACES

Fair, The Donkey

Contributed by Katrina Webb, a Donkey Sanctuary supporter

We have visited The Donkey Sanctuary for years – it was one of the places my husband and I visited during our first Christmas together in England – but this year's Fair was the first I had attended.

My husband expressed an interest in walking around the upper fields and, as I was quite tired from earlier exertions at the tombola tables, I found a seat by the hospital paddocks. I watched the recuperating donkeys as they went about the important business of grazing, while nonchalantly keeping an eye on all the activities around them. With some amusement I noticed how they would present themselves at the fence to be patted, then wander off for some grazing before casually wandering back towards the fence again.

A kind-looking elderly gentleman walked slowly and stiffly towards the hospital paddocks and, when he reached the fence, he leaned heavily on it, putting his sticks aside. Something about him reminded me of my grandfather. The nearest donkey, who had just tolerated a very great deal of boisterous patting from a large and excited family, lifted his head from the grass. He looked at the old man, blinked his great brown eyes slowly and nodded his head up and down. After a moment he walked purposefully towards the fence, positioning himself alongside the old man, and pressed his side against the railings. The old man reached out a trembling hand and patted the dear shaggy face, placing his other hand on the donkey's neck to balance himself. And there they stood, the old man and the old donkey.

I thought again of my grandfather, and the very large, cherished photo of him I had to leave behind in Australia. It showed Grandpa on his own horse, the Waler he took with him when he travelled halfway around the world as one of the Australian Light Horse Regiment in the First World War. The tall brown gelding saved his life twice, but Grandpa had to make the most heart-wrenching decision of his life in Egypt. The war was finally over, and the courageous men of the Light Horse who had somehow survived were going home. But their brave mounts were not. Only one token Waler, 'Sandy' was ever brought back to Australia. The commanding officers gave orders that the war horses had to be left in Egypt to their fate. My grandfather, distraught at what the future would hold for his brave and much-loved war horse, took him into the desert, gave him all the bread from his own rations, and shot him. My grandfather never got over it.

At that time, in that place, there was no sanctuary. As the old man gently stroked the donkey's ears, I thought how my Grandpa would have loved The Donkey Sanctuary. Here is a place of sanctuary that was denied to the war horses at the end of the First World War. Here is a place where donkeys can enjoy their final years in peace and comfort. And a place of forgiveness, where donkeys who may have been mistreated terribly in the past still walk trustingly up to people to be patted.

As happy families bustled around the stalls, displays and paddocks, and the donkeys alternately grazed or pressed close to the fences to be patted, the deeper message of The Donkey Sanctuary was clear: the old man patting the old donkey smiled, and the donkey pressed closer towards him.

The Summer Fair

Fostering scheme

- The Donkey Sanctuary fosters out pairs of donkeys or mules to suitable homes around the country. However, they remain the property of the charity at all times.
- Foster homes need a minimum of one acre of grazing for two donkeys.
- A shelter or stable is required, as well as hard standing, good fencing, shade from the sun and a constant supply of fresh drinking water.
- Foster owners take on the cost of the donkeys, including dental care and veterinary costs. Ongoing costs include flu vaccinations (annually) and tetanus (bi-annually), annual dental checks, farriery (every six to eight weeks), insurance, feed and bedding.
- All prospective foster owners attend one of the Sanctuary's free 'Donkey Care Induction Days' held throughout the country.

Kurt and Fabia receive lots of love and affection from their foster owner

- Support and advice is always available and foster homes will be visited three to four times a year by one of the Sanctuary's Welfare Officers.
- For more details visit our website: www.thedonkeysanctuary.org.uk

France – our work there

- We operate a small licensed holding base in France, where up to eight rescued donkeys can be taken into care. Janet Lemmy, who runs the holding base also runs her own rescue centre and was previously a Welfare Officer for The Donkey Sanctuary.
- We have used Janet's base as a resting point for donkeys rescued from all over Europe, especially the donkeys rescued from Naples Zoo in 2004.

DONKEYS

Genie

Genie and her male companion, Merlin, came into our care in September 2002 when their previous owner was no longer able to care for them. During their admission medical it was established that Genie was in foal, so we began to keep a watchful eye on her and, on the morning of Friday 28th March 2003, little Ronda was born in our Clifford Smith barn. She was named in recognition of the loyal and dedicated service of Ron Smith, a member of staff who had been with us for nineteen years and was due to retire that day. After a few anxious hours our skilled veterinary staff reported that Ronda was fit and healthy and was suckling well.

Genie used to be very naughty to handle but nowadays she's very friendly and acts more like a dog! At Paccombe Farm she is the first donkey everyone gets to know, as she charges through the barn when she hears voices and looks as though she's going to attack, but she's just looking for attention and she nudges with her nose until she's noticed! She loves to be cuddled and have a well-placed kiss on the end of her nose. She puts her head on your shoulder asking you to stroke her face and scratch her ears, paying particular attention to the area around her eyes. The staff at Paccombe Farm love her, including the volunteer workers, most of whom go to see her before going home.

Genie has a friend called Jo Jo Ward who adores her! Genie is often seen wandering around the yard minding her own business with Jo Jo hot on her heels. This friendship has become particularly strong since Jo Jo had laminitis and Genie became her stable mate for a few weeks. They were friends before but never really minded being apart for any reason, but now it appears they've decided they would like to be friends forever.

Genie

George

We have a dedicated team of thirty-eight Welfare Officers through-out the UK and Ireland, so we are able to investigate reports of cruelty or neglect very quickly. Our Regional Welfare Officer, Molly Lloyd, was alerted by the RSPCA to the plight of a donkey called George. George was found lying down in an exposed field and he had great difficulty in moving, as his hooves were long and twisted. Although he had a very thick coat, Molly could feel that his ribs were prominent. The owner was persuaded to sign George over to us, and he was immediately loaded up and taken to our nearest base. He was more than content to be put in a stable with deep straw and food, as well as plenty of fresh, clean water, as he was extremely thirsty. Presumably, because he was so weak and his feet were so painful he had not been able to reach food and water. George is now a very happy donkey and is guaranteed a home and expert loving care for life.

George loves his new life in New Barn at the Sanctuary

Georgie

Georgie had been abandoned but, unlike most donkeys that are abandoned and left to roam the countryside, Georgie had been tied to a 'Stop' sign on a main road just outside a village in the Paphos area of Cyprus. We don't know if his owner no longer wanted him due to some very nasty infected wounds on one of his legs but it was obvious that the rope used to tether him was far too tight. So tight, in fact, that he could barely walk.

Georgie can walk much better nowadays

Because he was on a main road the traffic was very close to him and, out of fear, he ran round and round the post until he ran out of rope. There was no water for him and he couldn't reach the nearby grass. Consequently he became very weak and simply lay down and was on the verge of giving up. The weather was awful – cold and heavy rain and so when we got to him he was in a very sorry state.

Fortunately The Donkey Sanctuary (Cyprus) Welfare Officer lives in Paphos and was able to take food and water to him until the trailer arrived. By the time we got there, Georgie was up on his feet. On their return they were able to stop at the Sanctuary vet's clinic so that the infected leg could be looked at and the first treatment administered, including antibiotic injections.

As is often the case, Georgie was rather bewildered when he arrived to find lots of other donkeys! After a lot of medical care, good food and a lot of TLC his leg recovered well, although he will always bear the scars of his injuries to remind us of how close he came to death.

Grumps, Donks and Jenny

On 31st July 2003 I was absolutely horrified to hear from our Regional Welfare Officer, Molly Lloyd, that she had been called by the RSPCA, whose inspector had visited a home as a result of a complaint about six dogs and thirteen puppies. As the Inspector couldn't find anyone at home he walked round to the buildings at the rear of the house where, to his horror, he found five ponies and three donkeys in 'indescribable conditions'. I quote from Molly as follows:

'We went down the track to the equines and I was appalled by what I saw. Across the front of a hay barn were some sheep hurdles and a metal gate. Muck had banked up to the top of the hurdles and gate, and only a tiny gap between the gate and the post enabled us to enter. To my left, tied to a girder, was an almost albino filly, about two years old. Loose and in a filthy rug was an old pony of about 14hh, score condition 5. About two and a half feet higher up on my left was a black colt, about two years old, in a pen made of sheep hurdles. His feet were extremely long, turning up and curling back towards his fetlock joints. He was standing as though he was trying to take the weight off his front end and was slightly tucked up. In the middle were two mare donkeys, one very old with overgrown and badly twisted feet and one quite young whose feet had been trimmed in the previous few days by a non-practising farrier. I climbed up the 'muck heap' to examine the donkeys more closely and whilst doing this I felt something chewing the toe of my boot. I looked down and, to my horror, saw a donkey stallion that was in a place I could only describe as a 'black hole'. He could just reach my foot if he stretched his neck and head right up the side of the muck heap that was containing him. His feet were extremely long and he had great difficulty walking as his back feet tangled up in each other.

We then went to see the other ponies. One was on what I can only describe as a plinth of muck about five feet high. She was unable to turn around, lie down or get down. Her feet were extremely long, although her bodily condition was good. To her left was a shed containing a colt of about three years. He was standing on a muck pile of about five feet (his feet were at my eye level and I am five feet, five inches tall). His feet were horrific. His back feet extended about ten inches from his leg and then curled. His front feet curled round and round like giant conch shells. He could not lift his head above the height of his withers as he was standing too close to the corrugated roof.'

The muck had to be dug out to form a ramp for the animals to walk out. Sadly one pony had to be put down, as its feet were so bad it couldn't walk. The others were given immediate remedial farriery treatment, and the World Horse Welfare (formerly The International League for the Protection of Horses) was able to take the ponies away, while the three donkeys were transported to The Donkey Sanctuary. Our farrier continued to work on the donkeys' feet. Donks, Grumps and Jenny all responded well to treatment and will be safe and secure for the rest of their lives.

I visited Donks, Grumps and Jenny soon after they arrived and, despite the ordeal they had suffered, they came up to me and I must admit that tears came

The rescue

to my eyes as I gently stroked them. They were so trusting, and they welcomed my visit. How wonderful donkeys are – I wish some of us human beings had their humility and their faith. During their period of isolation it became clear that, although Grumps and Jenny were good friends, they were not particularly close to Donks, who now lives happily at Brookfield Farm. Sadly Jenny died the following year.

Grumps was found to be in foal and, on 6th March 2004, she gave birth to a beautiful gelding, who we named Ponk. (see his story under 'P') Thank goodness she didn't have to give birth on that great pile of dung! I shudder to think what would have happened to the foal, and am doubtful that it would have survived.

Both we and the RSPCA were very distressed to find it was not possible to bring a prosecution against the owner of the animals for various reasons. Frankly, we were appalled that this could go unpunished without legal action being taken – if only to secure a court order to prevent owners such as this from keeping animals in the future.

Gwalior

Donkeys work alongside some of the poorest people in Indian society as labourers in the construction industry – carrying bricks, sand and other heavy supplies. These donkeys and mules work with small family groups. In some

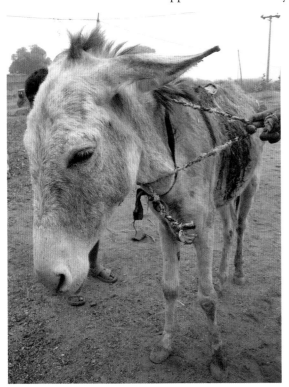

places, entire families migrate with their donkeys to areas where there is building work or brick making. The donkeys working in the brick kilns in particular have a really hard life, working long hours and carrying heavy loads of bricks and sand. The families live on site in makeshift tents. Some of the children work; some look after their younger siblings and some help to take care of their family's donkeys when they are not working.

Gwalior was seen by members of our staff when they took their mobile unit to Rama brick kiln in Gwalior (hence this donkey's name). His wounds were treated by our vet and he was given injections to help him fight off infection. Sadly as his owners were very poor he was not properly rested because they put him to work wherever they could find it and he was constantly on the move. His owners did, however, accept advice on his care and how to avoid problems for him in the future.

Gwalior

DONKEY FACTS, PEOPLE AND PLACES

Greece – our work there

- The Donkey Sanctuary began working in Greece in 2005 when a group of fourteen donkeys were relinquished in Athens. A holding base was set up in Trikala to house them and they have since been joined by more donkeys, many of whom have suffered through being unwanted, abandoned or been mistreated working animals. Thirty-three donkeys are currently at the holding base.
- Sanctuary representatives visit the licensed holding base regularly to ensure that the donkeys are being well cared for.
- Working donkeys and events using donkeys are monitored throughout mainland Greece and the Greek Islands.
- The Donkey Sanctuary has waged a campaign for many years on behalf of the donkeys and mules used as taxis for tourists on the island of Santorini.

Donkeys at our holding base in Trikala

Santorini

For many years the donkeys and mules on the Greek Island of Santorini have suffered from abuse – and are still doing so today. For years, unknowing tourists have used the 'burro taxis' to get up the 587 steps set into the side of the cliff from the ferry port to the town of Thira. This is causing the animals much suffering. They wear poorly fitting harnessing (exacerbated by overweight riders), are often cruelly treated by their masters, and the provision of food, water and shelter is rarely satisfactory.

The Donkey Sanctuary has tried to work alongside the municipality of Thira and the donkey masters to make improvements for the donkeys and mules – to no avail. During 2009 the charity was led to believe that significant improvements would be made with the full support of the municipality and the donkey masters, who had agreed to work to a special code of practice designed to protect the donkeys' most basic welfare needs. However we have continued to receive complaints from holiday-makers, and spot checks on the animals have revealed that standards slip whenever representatives from the Sanctuary are not on the island.

Laden donkeys climbing the 587 steps on Santorini

DONKEYS

Hannah

Hannah is a pretty white mare, born in 1997, and she arrived at The Donkey Sanctuary in 2003. Due to illness her owner could no longer give Hannah the love and care she had enjoyed. She was the 8,760th donkey to be taken into the Sanctuary's care. She is quiet and gentle and loves human company, so she was soon 'snapped up' to work at the EST Centre near Manchester. Hannah seems to have the ability to read just what her rider wants to do as they take part in the arena games, and the children love her. She is also one of the donkeys on the Adoption Scheme.

The staff at the Centre have started to use a new method of training for the donkeys, which is called 'clicker training'. Hannah was used as an example to the other donkeys, as apparently she was trained this way when she was young. She is proud to demonstrate her skills to donkeys and staff alike!

Hannah seems to be asking, 'What's going on?'

Hansel and Gretal

After the death of Miss Philpin (see her story under 'P') and my surprise legacy of 204 donkeys, one of the worst jobs was tracing the animals that were not at the Sanctuary near Reading. I was soon informed of the whereabouts of one group of twenty-two who were apparently being cared for by a couple to whom I shall, for obvious reasons, refer to as Mr and Mrs Smith. The donkeys had been 'boarded out' to them, for which Miss Philpin promised to pay them two pounds per animal per week. Now they wanted the large sum of money they said Miss Philpin owed them.

I called round to see them and they agreed that I could send a lorry to collect the donkeys. I called at a difficult time, as they were just putting Sunday lunch on the table, so I didn't see the donkeys, who were in a field some distance away. I knew I would see them on their arrival the next day.

At the time, Judith Forbes, who was running a Countryside Park three miles from my home, was renting me a large modern barn for the larger loads of arrivals and it was she who phoned me. Normally a very calm person, she sounded desperate. 'Betty, the lorry has arrived, but please come at once. The donkeys are in the most appalling condition.'

I jumped into my car with Rosalind de Wesselow, who was (and still is) one of the Trustees of The Donkey Sanctuary and we drove to the Park. The whole group were in a dreadful state. Two tiny ones were huddled together, barely able to stand, eyes dull with starvation – walking skeletons covered in matted hair, full of lice and covered in sores.

We had to carry them into a little stable that Mrs Forbes immediately offered us. We laid them down gently on the deep straw. I just could not believe people could allow any animal to get into such a state. I was so angry I rang the RSPCA and asked them to come out at once, as I was determined to bring a prosecution against Mr and Mrs Smith.

I named the two little donkeys Hansel and Gretal, as for them it must have felt like being in a fairy tale. The vet's report on Hansel read, 'This donkey is in extremis – showing severe distress due to starvation. His condition is appalling and he will be lucky to live. No disease apparent.' On Gretal the comments were, 'Very, very poor – breathing laboured and heavy, a walking skeleton, full of lice, starved almost to death.'

Hansel, Gretal and three others from the group were suffering so badly from starvation that they had to be hand fed throughout the day and night. Gradually their strength returned and after nine days they could stand unaided. Only then were they fit to be brought back to me at Slade House Farm, where it was so much easier to do the night feeds that were still essential. They were still terrified of being handled, but they were beginning to know us. As they improved I was able to start the long job of gently clipping away the matted hair and getting rid of the deeply embedded lice. Even though I wore a headscarf and tightly fitting clothes there was still a ring of lice around the bath when I got out. Ugh!

With the vet's help the sores were treated and began to heal, and Hansel and Gretal settled down. They had to be rugged up every night as the evenings got colder and we fitted an infrared light overhead to keep them warm. It was such a joy to see them roll in the sanded area, which had a liberal sprinkling of louse powder in it to prevent further infestation. They began to enjoy life at last.

I had written to Mr and Mrs Smith telling them what I thought of their care of the donkeys and adding that we intended to bring a prosecution through the RSPCA. To my horror on receipt of the letter Mr Smith phoned me to say he was going to take the donkeys back. He said he was sure we wouldn't pay the money Miss Philpin owed him and was most unpleasant. I told him the donkeys were not at my address, but were elsewhere, but he said he was coming anyway and would find them. I phoned the police, as I was really frightened he would turn up. The police were wonderful, particularly when I showed them Hansel and Gretal. They stayed on the alert until such time as I realised the man wasn't going to carry out his threat.

The law took its course and in December I, along with our vet and the RSPCA inspector went along to the court. When I heard Mr and Mrs Smith's evidence I couldn't believe it! The donkeys, according to them, had been groomed, fed and cared for daily. Fortunately the photographs we had taken along showed the truth; the couple were found guilty under the Protection of Animals Act 1911 and fined the maximum penalty of fifty pounds. Considering that four of the group of twenty-two died within two years as a direct result of the starvation they had been subjected to, it didn't seem a very heavy fine.

Gretal progressed steadily, but Hansel took much, much longer. After two years with us he seemed set to develop fully, but then we nearly had a disaster. Although a gelding, he still had male instincts and one day tried to ride Gretal. To our horror he dislocated his hip and the vet had quite a job to help him. After that he was a little more cautious! Sadly both Hansel and Gretal are no longer with us, but they live forever in my memory.

Hansel and Gretal were a sorry sight when they arrived

Happy Harry

Happy Harry was found wandering around, looking very worried, near the village of Prastio in the Limassol district of Cyprus early in November 2008 by a lady who used to foster two of our donkeys. Fortunately she had a stable and a

Happy Harry

field to put him in while we, with the help of the police and the mayor of the village, tried to find out who he belonged to. Although she obviously didn't know his name, because of his lovely nature and his apparent gratitude at being treated so well, the lady named him Happy Harry! The owner couldn't be traced, so Happy Harry was brought to The Donkey Sanctuary (Cyprus). As is often the case, no one came to claim him and so after his isolation period he joined one of our groups. He looked quite surprised at meeting lots of other donkeys as we think he had spent most of his life on his own.

Happy Harry is around eighteen years old and we believe he was a working donkey that the owner no longer wanted. His feet were very overgrown and he has been very fat in the past, judging by the large fat roll he has on his neck! A bit of dieting has got some of the fat off his body but the roll on his neck is unlikely to disappear. Happy Harry has been a paragon of virtue ever since he arrived! The lady who found him still comes up to see him and give him a groom and a cuddle, which he loves.

Heidi

The vets at The Donkey Sanctuary were deeply concerned about a large white donkey mare named Silver who had come into our care on 15th February 2005. Her owner felt that the Sanctuary was the best place for her, as she had a large growth (known as a sarcoid) on her udder – and she was in foal.

Unfortunately donkeys are rather prone to developing sarcoids, which can occur anywhere on the body, with surgery sometimes being the only option. In Silver's case it was obvious that she would have to be operated on, but certainly not while she was so heavily in foal. One of her teats was affected, leaving only one completely clear for the new foal to use.

I voiced my concerns to Glen Gardiner, manager of the New Arrivals Unit as to whether or not the foal would be able to suckle and in response he took me to see the arrangements that had been made in case it couldn't. Preparations had been made by staff to stay overnight if necessary, so that the foal could be bottle-fed every two hours, and a kettle was on hand to make up fresh supplies of a special milk formula to give the new-born foal vital nutrients. I was moved to see the dedication of the staff – in fact one of my biggest delights is that every member of staff is dedicated to ensuring that the donkeys come first, second and third!

Glen rang me on Thursday morning to say he thought the birth was imminent, as Silver was producing milk. If she hadn't foaled by the end of the day he was arranging for the security officer to call in every couple of hours to check quietly if anything was happening. Donkeys are amazing animals and like to keep their foaling private – if interfered with just before the birthing process they can hold off for at least another week!

I was just dozing off to sleep at five past eight in the evening (I have to be up very early to start my day's work!) when the phone rang. The foal had been born! I arrived about five minutes later and quietly watched the beautiful pure white foal as she tried to stand. I was amazed to see her legs; they were the longest I've seen on a foal in all my years of caring for donkeys – so long, in fact, that they seemed incapable of holding her up, and she kept collapsing with legs flying in all directions!

Alex, our senior clinical vet, accompanied by her family, arrived to check that all was well with mother and baby. By this time the foal had managed to stand up, her long legs helping her to find the only accessible teat almost immediately, though she was still too unsteady to suckle. Alex's eldest daughter was entranced, with her face pressed to the bars of the fence and unwilling to take her eyes off the foal. In response to my question she told me that her name was Heidi. 'Would you like to let the foal share your name?' I asked. Without taking her eyes off the foal she nodded. 'Right then – she will be called Heidi!' I could swear the foal twitched her ears in agreement, and Silver gave a little snort as she nuzzled her beautiful new baby.

Fortunately Silver was able to feed her foal adequately, despite a few difficulties, and six months later, when Heidi was weaned, the sarcoid was successfully removed.

Heidi with her mother, Silver

Hercules

Hercules had been taken in by The Donkey Sanctuary (Cyprus) former owners, Patrick and Mary Skinner. He came into care in 2002 as a three-month-old foal. His mother had died so he had been hand-reared and, as a consequence, had been rather spoilt. He didn't understand that he was a donkey and the people caring for him were humans – he thought it was great fun to climb all over people and generally do what he liked!

Over the years Hercules has gradually learned to live with other donkeys and his behaviour has improved, although he can still be very naughty! The grooms kept finding the door to the feed store open and were blaming each other for not shutting it properly. We then discovered it was Hercules who was managing to open it by banging his hoof against the door to loosen the bolt! The quickest solution was to tie the door up with string but he soon learned how to undo that. We then arranged for some special 'donkey proof' stable bolts to be sent over from The Donkey Sanctuary in the UK. This solved the

problem – or so we thought! Once again the staff started accusing each other of not shutting the stable gates inside the barn, especially as both gates had the special bolts on them. You've guessed it – Hercules! We really don't know how he does it because sometimes even we struggle to open them!

He is always up to mischief and if you suddenly find your grooming kit or a head collar missing you know who has run off with it. Some of his friends in the paddock do get a little fed up with him wanting to play with them! Although he can be a bit of a handful sometimes, the staff love him dearly.

Hercules looks as though he's up to mischief!

Hope Makedonia

In 2003 my son, Paul, organised a rescue in Greece when he heard that a twenty-eight-year-old female donkey had been attacked with shovels by louts, causing injuries from the top of her neck to the root of her tail. They finished by cutting off both ears about three inches from their base. She had been rescued and was being cared for by the owners of a dog rescue centre.

She was named Makedonia, as this was the name of the street where she was found, but we felt she should be re-named and asked our supporters to send us their ideas. We received over 1,300 suggestions and, as 'Hope' was by far the most popular name she was re-named Hope Makedonia.

Hope Makedonia, with Paul Svendsen, Director of European Operations. She was one of the first donkeys rescued in continental Europe

Annie Brown, the Sanctuary's General Farms Manager went to Greece to organise the paperwork so that Hope could be moved from Greece to Spain where, at the time, we were in the process of buying a farm to set up a Spanish Sanctuary. She tells the story:

> 'I couldn't believe how gentle and docile Hope was, considering the awful treatment she had received by some young thugs who had chopped off her ears with a shovel and scraped the shovel along her back taking off the skin and hair.
>
> Getting the veterinary certificate for fitness to travel was quite an ordeal as it was a public holiday and all the official offices were closed, so I had to organise it all early in the morning on the day the lorry was due to leave. The Sanctuary's driver, Brian, drove Hope, together with her companion and four other rescued donkeys, back to Spain – a long and arduous journey through Kosovo and into the (then) war zone with an army escort.'

The donkeys were taken to our holding base in Toulouse in southern France and when, later that year, El Refugio del Burrito was opened in Spain, they were moved there, where they continue to receive the care and attention they deserve, although Hope sadly died in August 2010.

DONKEY FACTS, PEOPLE AND PLACES

Honours

I have been so fortunate in life and really appreciate the honours that have been bestowed on me. I owe a great deal of thanks to all my staff – from the earliest days I have been blessed with wonderful helpers, without whom my work may well have gone unnoticed. As well as notable honours, I have also been awarded many gifts in the countries I've visited, some of which have been quite amusing.

The MBE

The MBE is my most prized honour, awarded to me in 1980. At that time my work at The Donkey Sanctuary was beset with difficulties – including the donkeys bequeathed to me by Miss Philpin, I now had over three hundred in my care, with more coming in all the time, and by April 1981 I was in the throes of buying another farm to house them all. I was told of the award late in December 1980 and, together with my husband, Niels, and two of my children, Clive and Sarah, I went to Buckingham Palace the following April to receive it. What an experience! We'd all bought new clothes for the occasion and Niels and Clive had hired grey top hats which looked superb. I must confess that I was extremely nervous as we drove through the gates of the palace.

My MBE

I need not have worried, though. The equerry placed those to receive awards in order and explained what we had to do. He told us that when our names were called, we had to stop in front of the Queen, do a curtsy (men had to bow), walk forward five paces, receive our award, only speak when spoken to, reverse five paces and then walk through the exit, where we would receive our medals. As we stood outside the main chamber the occasion became almost too much for me and I realised that I quite desperately needed to 'spend a penny'! The equerry seemed rather disturbed when I told him my predicament but I was rushed to what appeared to be a glass panel down the side of the chamber. This was in fact a secret door; he pushed it in a certain way and I went into a small room with an elaborate washbasin and an even more spectacular toilet. I realised that I could, indeed, be sitting on the royal throne! I just managed to rejoin the line as we were led forward, seeing Lady Diana Spencer sitting at the back of the hall as we passed, obviously having been given the opportunity to watch before she married Prince Charles.

There was a tremendous atmosphere as the Queen began bestowing the honours on those in front of me. I can hardly remember following the instructions, but I do remember the surprised expression on the Queen's face when she asked, 'And what is your work, my dear?' and I replied, 'Donkeys, Your Majesty!' A look of amazement crossed her face and then I explained I also worked with donkeys and children with special needs, at which she smiled at me and said, 'Well done'!

Niels, Clive and Sarah joined me when the ceremony was over, and together we stood in the Palace Yard having our photographs taken. I was highly amused when I looked at Clive and Niels as, by mistake, they were wearing

After the ceremony. Note Niels and Clive wearing the wrong hats!

each other's hats. Niels' was perched on top of his head while Clive's was firmly down to his eyebrows! It was certainly a day I'll never forget!

An honour from Nigeria

In 1990 with my friend June, we travelled to Nigeria at the invitation of Dr Onoviran who had a senior position in the Government Veterinary Service and was Registrar of the Nigerian Veterinary Council. Dr Onoviran had asked for our advice on donkey welfare, as he was sure that anthelmintics (medi-cation to eradicate worms) were the answer to the problems for donkeys in Nigeria. Little did we realise that half of the time would be spent being introduced to VIPs in each little village we passed through as we travelled from Lagos to the north. We grew more and more frustrated as the days passed, as we saw hardly any donkeys.

There were some funny incidents, however. Each area in Nigeria has its own Emir (the equivalent of royalty for the area) and we were invited to visit the Emir of Keffi. We were ushered into the Royal Headquarters, having been pre-warned that we should curtsy and call the Emir 'Your Highness'. We weren't prepared for the scribes and village elders sitting along the side of the room, nor the bodyguards dressed in brilliant red, green and yellow long-flowing robes. Our group, which included Dr Onoviran, his veterinary surgeon col-leagues, the Keffi Chief Veterinary Officer and his Agricultural Officers, was seated on large chairs down the left-hand side of the room. Each made a speech in turn and then I was asked to speak. I pointed out how we hoped to be able to help the Nigerians by improving the health of their don-keys and extending their lifespan, thereby increasing their working capacity. The Emir asked me to step forward as he wished to make a presentation and, completely unsuspecting I stood in front of him wondering what was coming next. A large leather and straw hat was passed to the Emir who, with great ceremony, placed it on my head. I realised that this was a moment of great seriousness and importance, and I was indeed very honoured. Unfortunately the honour hadn't been bestowed on women before; men usually have larger heads than women and in Nigeria a man would probably be wearing a turban. The hat slid down over my eyes and rested on my nose! There was a moment of embarrassing silence and, lifting my head to peer out beneath the hat I could see that June was convulsed with laughter. In fact the whole of my group was finding it highly amusing! I couldn't help bursting out laughing myself and was very relieved to find that the Emir had also found it funny – so much so that he had to sit down as he was laughing so much.

Me wearing that hat!

In the end we found all the donkeys were north of Kano – in fact over one million in a very small area between there and Nigeria's border with the Republic of Niger. We dosed all we possibly could with anthelmintic and returned home having promised to try to help further in the future.

An Egyptian award

By 1992 we were expanding our work around the world, visiting countries to establish the need for setting up mobile clinics and treating the cruelly over-worked donkeys for parasites and terrible wounds free of charge. I had been worried by the plight of working donkeys in Egypt, and a meeting with Dr Mourad Ragheb in 1987, originally a vet for the World Health Organisation, had convinced me to start work in the Cairo area, with Dr Ragheb in charge. I had been asked to give a paper at a Conference in Cairo, organised by Transport Animal Welfare and Studies (TAWS) on the subject of working animals, and we'd also agreed to fund three overseas vets to give papers on our work for donkeys abroad.

Sitting in the Conference Hall the morning after we'd arrived, we listened as the President of the Egyptian Veterinary Association, Dr Shalash, gave his opening address. He then followed by announcing that he was awarding presentations for merit. I was amazed when my name was called out and, as I approached the platform I vaguely heard him saying that the award was 'for her work on donkey welfare throughout the world'. I was given a certificate and an enormous medal was placed round my neck, with a picture of a large buffalo and the inscription 'Egyptian Veterinary Association for Buffalo Development – Science Pioneer Prize.' I didn't like to mention that buffalos are not the same as donkeys!

My Egyptian 'Buffalo' award!

Doctor of Veterinary Medicine and Surgery

My award of the Honorary Degree of Veterinary Medicine and Surgery (DVMS) from the University of Glasgow in 1992 opened many doors to government departments and veterinary universities in various parts of the world. In some of the most remote areas of developing countries being a woman was a drawback, but being *Doctor* Svendsen gave my advice on donkey welfare much more kudos with the authorities and local people.

The graduation ceremony at the university was amazing. Our academic procession was led by pipers and the sound of a delightful organ concerto greeted us as we entered the great Bute Hall. I felt wonderful in my beautiful robe, which was a bright red denoting a veterinary honour. I was presented for my degree by Professor Norman Wright, Professor of Veterinary Anatomy as, sadly, Max Murray, my original presenter was unable to do so, due to illness. I sat on an ornate chair on the dais while he said, 'Mr Chancellor, by authority of the Senate, I present to you this person on whom the Senate desires you to confer the Honorary Degree of Doctor of Veterinary Medicine and Surgery. As this is the 130th anniversary of the Foundation of the Veterinary School I would now ask you to confer this honour on Elisabeth Doreen Svendsen, only the second ever to be awarded by the Faculty of Veterinary Medicine.' I then knelt on the stool below the Chancellor, who sat on what I can only describe as a high throne overlooking the proceedings. He then stood and, placing a round purple hat on my head, intoned several words of Latin, after which my hood was placed over my head and I became a doctor.

Being 'doctored'!

One of my awards from the AVS

Association of Veterinary Students

As Administrator of The Donkey Sanctuary I was often asked to give talks to veterinary students. I enjoyed these events, as I felt that the students would at least learn a little about donkey welfare. To make the talks more interesting I used to ask my staff to put together little sealed bags, each one numbered and containing items which had the same feel and consistency of items relating to donkeys and their welfare. They ranged from edible equine foods, medication and parasites. I asked the students to pass these around and every now and then I would stop talking, pick someone to feel a bag and ask what he or she thought was inside. It was amusing to hear the imaginative guesswork, especially with regard to my favourite – a dung sample represented by marshmallows!

I was delighted to receive three awards over the years. This lovely cut glass vase has inscribed on its base, 'Hill's Pet Nutrition's individual award for service to the Association of Veterinary Students 1995'.

Equine Welfare Award

In 2007 the British Equine Veterinary Association (BEVA) held their forty-sixth Congress in Edinburgh, and in this year I was honoured to be the recipient of their Equine Welfare Award, sponsored by the Blue Cross. Receiving these awards always demands a short speech in front of varying sizes of audience. I had written a brief response but, before it was my turn, Blue

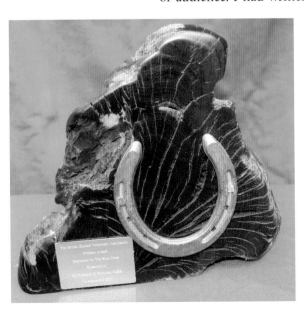

Cross's Chief Executive, John Rutter, explained to the audience why this award was to be given to me. Becoming more and more concerned as I listened, I realised his introduction covered most of what I intended to say – if he'd had my notes he couldn't have done better! I'm always terribly nervous before lecturing or speaking in public and I could feel disaster looming. I was saved by the award itself – a small, silver horseshoe set on an attractive piece of bog oak. Happily I quickly managed to relate the background of bog oak to Ireland, to the conditions faced by many donkeys in that country, and how our work in Ireland is helping to alleviate the situation. I was saved!

Equine Welfare Award

Accolades from other charities

Donkey Breed Society

I was delighted to be made an Honorary Life Vice President of the Donkey Breed Society (DBS) in 1997 and I was nominated for inclusion on the Roll of Honour.

Lord Erskine Award

In June 2001 I was delighted to hear that I was to be given The Lord Erskine Award by the RSPCA for my work with animals. Receiving the award wasn't straightforward, though, as I'd broken my ankle earlier that month and movement wasn't easy! Luckily my nephew, Peter Feather, was staying with me at the time and he drove me to Newport in South Wales to receive the award at the RSPCA's Annual General Meeting. I was presented with a lovely engraved glass plaque and a citation. It was quite difficult balancing on one leg to receive it!

*The Lord Erskine
Award and Citation*

Doctor Honoris Causa

My latest honour was very kindly awarded to me by the University of Edinburgh. This was a degree of *Doctor Honoris Causa* given for my 'pioneering work in the care and welfare of donkeys throughout the world'.

I travelled to Edinburgh in November 2009 to be 'doctored' again! Once again the ceremony was wonderful, but I was very nervous, as I had to give a speech to the audience of over eight hundred people. As the students filed past to receive their degrees I was surprised to see one of The Donkey Sanctuary's vets, Alex Thiemann –there to receive her Masters Degree. Although I had been aware of her recent success I didn't know she was to receive it that day. Knowing that Alex, as well as my friend, June, was there I felt more confident – and even ended my speech with a slightly naughty story!

I was enormously grateful to University of Edinburgh for granting me this honorary degree. On top of the pleasure that helping the donkeys has given me over the years, it was wonderful to find others who are also keen to recognise the important contribution that donkeys have made to mankind. All the work that has been achieved over the years at The Donkey Sanctuary has given me great satisfaction and I am enormously proud of the staff and all our supporters, who work so hard to make life better for donkeys throughout the world.

Having now received two honorary degrees I can now be referred to as 'Doctor Doctor Svendsen'!

Becoming 'Doctor Doctor Svendsen'!

Taking the words from Dr Svendsen's mouth!

I was privileged to have been Chief Executive of The Blue Cross from 2001 until my retirement in 2008 – 'privileged' not just because this fine charity's mission was to improve the welfare of many animals – a cause close to my heart – but also because I had the joy of making many new friends and acquaintances, especially in like-minded animal charities. One of these new relationships which I particularly treasured was with Dr Elisabeth Svendsen, who founded The Donkey Sanctuary in 1969, registering as a charity four years later.

From time to time The Blue Cross has given awards to very special people who had shown exceptional dedication to the advancement of animal welfare. I had seen Betty's unique commitment to donkey welfare and in September 2007 I recommended to our Trustees that she would be a most worthy recipient of our Award for Outstanding Service to Equine Welfare. Without hesitation they enthusiastically endorsed the recommendation.

Of course, the Blue Cross Award is just one of many accolades and honours our heroine has received. However, if they could speak, the greatest plaudits would be from thousands upon thousands of donkeys from around the world. Betty, we salute you!

Contributed by John Rutter, Former Chief Executive of Blue Cross and since 2008 a Trustee of The Donkey Sanctuary

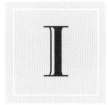

DONKEYS

Inky

In the 1990s The Donkey Sanctuary undertook a small breeding programme to preserve the endangered Poitou species (see more under 'P'). One of our big part-bred Poitou donkeys, Vicky, gave birth to Inky in June 1996. As you can see, he has Poitou characteristics; he's a huge donkey and has a matted, shaggy coat.

Inky, a splendid-looking donkey!

Iolanthe (right) with mother, Danielle (left)

Iolanthe

Again during the Poitou breeding programme, Marwell Zoo loaned the Sanctuary a pure-bred stallion named Theodore to mate with the charity's pure-bred donkey, Danielle. The result was Iolanthe, who was born in April 1996. Danielle and Iolanthe live together in the Poitou Barn at Slade House Farm.

Irene

Irene is a nineteen-year-old pretty skewbald donkey who lives with her mother, Judy Wren, at Paccombe Farm. They came into the care of the Sanctuary in 1992 and were later sent to a foster home in Wales. However, they had to be returned to the Sanctuary in 2006 due to the foster owner's ill health.

Although Irene is a very quiet donkey, she is very loving, and she's always ready for a cuddle from the grooms!

Irene

Islander

In October 1983 a very worried lady wrote to us to say she had heard there was an abandoned donkey in Ireland who had been left for eighteen years on a very small island inhabited only by sheep. The original human occupants had been moved by the government. The donkey had only received rudimentary care when shepherds visited and it was now, apparently, in some distress. Our Welfare Officers, despite every attempt, found that it was impossible to find a boat large enough to move the donkey during the winter but they managed to trace the owner, who agreed he would ensure that the donkey would receive as much help throughout the inclement months as was possible. It was then arranged with a local fisherman that, as soon as weather permitted, he and the Welfare Officers would go across and bring the donkey back to the mainland, which they did. The owner of the donkey was persuaded to sign the donkey over to the Sanctuary and, as soon as this was done, it was moved to a temporary home on the Irish mainland.

A vet was called immediately to the donkey, who we named Islander, to see if it would be kinder to put him down as he was in such a poor condition. However, the vet felt that, despite his lameness, poor condition and extensive body parasites, with the right care, Islander had the spirit and will to live and should be given a chance of life. It was decided to bring him back to the Sanctuary in Devon, carried in a specially adapted horse box, with veterinary inspections en route to ensure he was fit to continue. Luckily the sea was calm during the crossing and he arrived showing very little sign of travel stress. He was greeted by the usual bray of all the other donkeys and for the first time he lifted his head and looked round in wonder to see, not only the green fields but other donkeys – animals he'd never seen before – happily grazing. He very soon made friends with the other donkeys, whose company, no doubt, helped in Islander's full recovery.

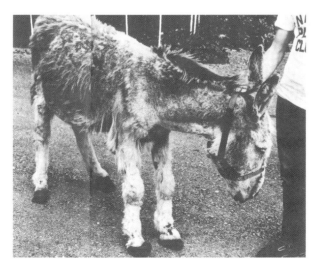

Islander

Ivor

In November 2009 eighteen rescued donkeys were signed over to The Donkey Sanctuary by the RSPCA as a result of its successful prosecution of their owner. Among the group it was found that five mares were already in foal, and one of them, Domino, gave birth to Ivor on 27th July 2010.

I'm sure you will agree that Ivor is absolutely gorgeous!

Ivor

DONKEY FACTS, PEOPLE AND PLACES

India – our work there

The Donkey Sanctuary began working with the Indian charity 'People For Animals' in 1998 and went on to set up The Donkey Sanctuary India (DSI) in 2002, a charity registered in India with its own board of trustees. We started with a rented office and mobile clinic based in Gurgaon which, until recently, was a rural area but is now one of Delhi's rapidly-developing new southern suburbs. We now also have bases in Ahmedabad (Gujarat state), Gwalior (Madhya Pradesh state), Sikar (Rajasthan state) and Solapur (Maharashtra state). In Ahmedabad our base is at a small farm which is also used as a training centre for staff in all our Indian bases and, increasingly, for external personnel and organisations. In all these locations, the professionally trained veterinary and community development and education staff are supported by various animal health workers whom we have trained ourselves.

Our teams in India visit rural villages, brick kilns, building sites and other centres of donkey work such as markets, all of which are fairly close to their bases, as well as attending special fairs and religious events which involve donkeys. Unlike Egyptian brick kilns where the donkeys pull cartloads of bricks, in India the carts are pulled by mules which are more valuable and better cared-for, while donkeys carry the bricks and building materials in 'soggis' – sacks slung across their backs. Another difference is that, while the donkey drivers in Egypt are men or young boys who live nearby and travel to the kilns, in India there are whole families living in makeshift camps near the kilns or construction areas, with men, women and children sharing the work. They are contracted to work for the season, and they cannot fulfil this obligation without their donkeys. Many of these families – 'the poorest of the poor' as one of our Indian team describes them – do their best to look after their donkeys with the minimal resources they have, and welcome the treatments and advice our team can offer them.

Our team based in Delhi has recently begun visiting some 'new' kilns in an area called Badli. This is just beyond the western edge of Delhi (as kilns are not allowed to be set up within the city itself), in the state of Haryana. We have been holding talks with the donkey owners to assess the donkeys' welfare needs and planning the best way of helping them, by improving the owners' knowledge and making the best possible use of the existing animal health services. We are now introducing an integrated welfare programme in this area and will look to extend this into other locations with serious donkey welfare problems, where our assessments indicate that we can make a significant difference.

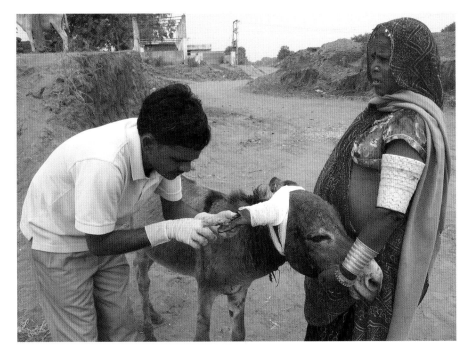

Udmi Ram, a Donkey Sanctuary India dresser, treating a donkey with a damaged ear in an Ahmedabad brick kiln

We also work with communities in other ways to reduce harm to donkeys. In Ahmedabad, donkeys were developing leg wounds caused by being hobbled with plastic string. We taught groups of women to make soft cotton hobbles from off-cuts of material. In Solapur, donkeys suffer colic after swallowing plastic bags while scavenging for food among the piles of litter in some of the streets. A lot of waste food is thrown into the street in plastic bags and we are trying to persuade people to put it into a special bin instead, from which it can be collected and given to the donkeys.

Story telling

The Donkey Sanctuary uses storytelling a great deal to help children to empathise with donkeys and see the difference between good and bad treatment.

Children working in brick kilns in Solapur have been helped to understand the benefits of treating working donkeys well, and were also given the opportunity to talk about their own working lives, at a one-day storytelling session held by Education Officer Suchitra Gadad with a group of children on their day off work. She used a puppet show to tell the story of Gopie and Bandu, two boys who have to work in the kilns with their donkeys. The cruel owner, Bandu, learns to feel empathy with his suffering donkeys when he himself is too ill to work and is beaten instead of receiving sympathy.

The story was used to get the children talking about their feelings for other living things, and whether humans and animals ever deserved to be beaten. Some of the children said they did hit their donkeys when they were too slow at work, because they themselves had to make a certain number of bricks each day. 'I told them that all this will change in a very slow way, but we mustn't give up and always go on with good things,' says Suchitra.

On the whole she found the discussions encouraging. 'I came to know that the new generation of children are very caring. They came up with positive methods to work with the donkeys.'

We use a range of techniques to educate donkey owners; storytelling works well for children, but we also use group discussions and videos, as in this picture

Ireland, The Donkey Sanctuary

Paddy Barrett and I first met in Cork in 1975, and he was as devoted to donkeys as I was! His family were so kind and hospitable, and I particularly remember the wonderful Irish breakfast I was served at their home – this comprised masses of ham cut fresh from the bone, with liberally buttered soda bread and two pints of coffee!

Paddy's father ran the Richard Martin Restfields in County Cork and the liaison between our two charities continued until 1987, when The Donkey Sanctuary took it over. In the meantime Paddy's father had died suddenly and Paddy himself took the reins, continuing as manager of The Donkey Sanctuary, Ireland. I knew that the donkeys would be in safe hands, and so it has been proved over the years!

Paddy Barrett with some of his charges

The **Sanctuary** is set in the beautiful rolling countryside of County Cork just outside the village of Liscarroll. Another farm, Hannigans, was purchased in 1996 to cope with the increasing number of donkeys coming into care. Despite this, the Irish Sanctuary is always full to capacity and some donkeys are occasionally brought over to the UK.

We have two full-time regional Welfare Officers whose sole responsibility is to co-ordinate our welfare work throughout Ireland and ensure that all reports of donkeys in trouble are investigated and dealt with as soon as possible.

To date, over 3,000 donkeys have been taken into care in Ireland.

Donkeys Sammy and Jack relax at the Irish Sanctuary

Italy – our work there

- Our work in Italy began in April 2004 when we rescued twenty-one donkeys from terrible conditions at a bankrupt zoo in Naples, the result of an urgent appeal from an Italian animal welfare association called Nata Libera.
- The donkey population in Italy is estimated in the region of 24,000 and they are used mainly for meat, which is a main ingredient in some salami and served up in restaurants as stews and in ravioli. They are also used for transportation in rural farming areas, animal assisted therapy and holiday trekking.
- Italy imports thousands of tons of equine meat from America every year and is the biggest European user of equine meat.
- In 2006 we established a subsidiary organisation called Il Rifugio degli Asinelli ONLUS as a charity in Italy which is running from our new farm in Sala Biellese, around 60 km North of Turin. This refuge is open to the public and will care for up to 250 donkeys when full; 113 have so far been taken into care.
- We are also addressing welfare issues in the country by investigating donkey breeding centres (for the production of milk and meat), markets and public events, such as races and fairs.
- On the farm we provide education and training to donkey owners and professionals and many schools bring their children for lectures on donkey welfare provided by the staff.
- We have several donkey grooming days during the year where we encourage local people to come and interact with the donkeys.

Donkeys at Il Rifugio degli Asinelli

DONKEYS

Jacinta

Jacinta was born at The Irish Donkey Sanctuary on 15th May 1997. Her mother Lorraine had been rescued earlier that year. She, along with twenty-one other donkeys had been living in a field with insufficient grazing for them all. The poor animals were so desperate that they were eating their own dung; they were so thin that it was necessary to drip-feed them when they first arrived, and the veterinary surgeon tending them said it was the worst case of cruelty and neglect he had ever witnessed. He was particularly concerned for Lorraine as she was heavily in foal. However her foal, Jacinta, arrived in perfect health.

Jacinta is strawberry roan in colour, and is a sweet and friendly donkey who enjoys lots of attention. She was one of the first donkeys to join the Adoption Scheme in 2001 and is still very popular with everyone – except when she brays. The staff say she has the loudest bray of all the donkeys at The Irish Sanctuary!

Jacinta is a real princess; she's proud of how beautiful she is as she moves graciously around in the adoption group paddock. Now thirteen years old she has become very bossy and likes to think she is in charge of the other adoption donkeys. She often pushes them to one side when she wants attention. See photo of Jacinta overleaf.

Jack

We were asked to collect a donkey from London for a very strange reason! The owner of a rag and bone cart in London's East End had lost his elderly donkey, and he had replaced him with a young stallion named Jack. However, things

were not the same. No-one could hear his calls for 'rags and bones' for, as soon as he shouted, Jack joined in – and Jack had a louder voice than his cockney owner! Strangely, Jack has been rather subdued since his arrival at the Sanctuary. Perhaps his castration operation has quietened him down a bit!

Jack made friends with a mule named Solly and they are both living happily at Town Barton Farm.

Janet Thorne

Karray came into our care with two other donkeys, one being a stallion. The owners were having difficulties, as the paddock was by a main road and there was a great risk the donkeys could get out. In addition the donkeys had long feet and had become difficult to handle. There was a strong suspicion that Karray could be in foal, so she was settled in a comfortable single stable with its

Jack

RIGHT *Janet Thorne –
a beautiful foal*

own little paddock in the New Arrivals Unit, and received lots of TLC and veterinary attention. Donkeys are great at hiding when the birth is imminent – sometimes we can tell but, as gestation can be anything from eleven to thirteen months, the donkey can keep the date a secret!

Little Janet Thorne was born early on Wednesday 6th May 2009, and I had no problem in naming her. The Donkey Sanctuary is so lucky to have many wonderful supporters, and Peter and Janet Thorne were two of the most dedicated, raising thousands of pounds for us as voluntary fundraisers by running stalls wherever and whenever they could, including Donkey Week and other special events both here and at our EST Centres. Very sadly Janet died in January 2009. Despite it being a very emotional time for him, Peter came along to Donkey Week again in May and was here when the little foal was born. So her choice of name was obvious and she will be a poignant reminder of a lovely lady. I'd like to share this photo of little Janet with you.

Jenny

Jenny was the five thousandth donkey to come into our care and she was in a very sad state when she arrived in 1991. She had been purchased as a foal by gypsies and had spent two years locked in a garage. She was then sold and her new owners kept her in their back garden until she was turned out with seven large horses. It was then that Jenny received a severe kick on her hock, which left a large scar. A local lady eventually found Jenny standing up to her stomach in mud. Although she had no land, in view of the donkey's plight, the lady agreed to have Jenny.

A friend kindly loaned her the use of a field until Jenny could be taken by an animal charity. Several charities were asked, but no home was available for her. Eventually someone mentioned The Donkey Sanctuary and Jenny's future was secure.

ABOVE *Jenny, number 5000!*

ABOVE RIGHT *Joseph can be a naughty donkey!*

Joseph

Joseph is one of Brookfield Farm's most charismatic donkeys. He once belonged to a retiring clergyman, who felt Joseph would be happier with other donkeys. He used to be friendly with a donkey named Bazil but now he appears to prefer his own company. He hates to be tied up while being groomed but, once he's been secured he will stand very still while he's being brushed, thoroughly enjoying the experience! He has a unique talent of opening gates and has been known to let his friends out of their yard area to go for a roam around the farm.

Jubilee

We were totally unprepared for the size of the mule we'd been asked to take into care in 1987! Jubilee was bred in 1977 in Newmarket. Her owner had worked with mules in the army and he loved them. He chose the mare carefully – her half brother, Rubstic, had won the Grand National in 1979. For the stallion he chose Éclair, one of the famous and, at that time endangered, Poitou donkeys.

Jubilee was magnificent; she stood 16.2 hands high (imagine a good-sized horse) but with enormous ears and the most beautiful eyes and muzzle. She

Jubilee, the gentle giant!

was very gentle although, according to the stable who took her in when her owner was no longer able to look after her, she was un-predictable when pulling a cart. It had been planned for her to go to a veterinary university where they would try various methods to get her in foal (normally mules are unable to reproduce) but, fortunately for her, a last minute change of heart and a little gentle persuasion from us saved her from experimentation. She spent many happy years with us and died in 2009.

Julie-Anne

Julie-Anne was born at the Irish Sanctuary on 2nd July 2007, a few months after her mother, Raynah, was rescued. She is a delightful, inquisitive, lively donkey who loves to play with the other donkeys that are available for adoption. She keeps them highly amused with her playful tricks, and is known for her frequent bursts of energy which result in her zooming around the paddock – sometimes even chasing the other donkeys. She also enjoys a good game of donkey football and the staff think she would make a great soccer player, although they don't think she's worked out the rules yet!

Julie-Anne

She has a sweet tooth, and is obviously in training to become a pick-pocket. One day a vet nurse felt something tug at her pocket and when she turned around Julie-Anne was trying to steal her polo mints!

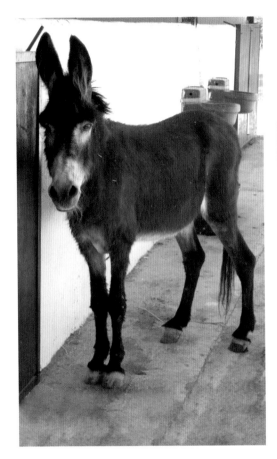

LEFT *Julito was given his name in honour of the well-known singer, Julio Iglesias (Julito means 'little Julio'). On arrival at the Sanctuary he soon began to demonstrate his musical abilities – braying loudly and often! We are proud to present this 'donkey divo' in our Spanish Adoption Scheme!'*

ABOVE *Julius has slimmed down since this photo was taken!*

Julius S

Julius came into The Donkey Sanctuary in 1998. The large 'growth' (as some people call it) around Julius's neck is, in fact, a fat reserve! (see photo above.) Julius had been grossly overfed before coming into our care, and he was in a really dangerous state on arrival. We find fat donkeys the most difficult to treat on arrival – they have obviously been very spoilt, and are going to find their new position very stressful. We always take a great deal of time and trouble to find out from their previous owners what special 'treats' the donkey is used to, and we then try to carry on with these treats, gradually weaning the donkey from them.

Julius received all the special care he needed until he had really settled down, and the vets were then able to start a very gradual slimming programme. At first Julius was very slow to move (although quick to eat!) and his saving grace came when one of our vets, Vicky Grove, introduced him to *her* donkey, Lucy. Julius fell in love immediately! Wherever Lucy went, Julius followed, and – guess what – he lost weight steadily!

DONKEY FACTS, PEOPLE AND PLACES

Jamie

Jamie was born nine weeks prematurely, weighing only three pounds eleven ounces, and his parents were devastated to learn soon afterwards that he had cerebral palsy. They were told by the doctors that he had brain damage and the tendons and ligaments in his legs were pulled tight, meaning that, even though he could 'commando crawl', he might never be able to walk. As he was unable to put weight on his legs, Jamie's hip sockets didn't develop properly, leaving one leg shorter than the other. He had to have an operation to pin and plate both of his hips. He also has very little vision in his left eye and there was concern of his being partly colour blind, although this has not been proved. Jamie's mother, June, told me:

'When Jamie was six months old I worked part-time in a residential home at weekends. My husband Peter, a lorry driver, looked after him while I worked, taking him out for long walks around the countryside where, one day, when he was about three years old, they came across The Donkey Sanctuary. Jamie loves animals and he was so excited to see all the donkeys in the fields.

After making some enquiries we arranged to take Jamie along to EST Sidmouth's Saturday Club. He was frightened at first and when some donkeys brayed close to him he put his fingers in his ears – he didn't like the noise! But as soon as we took him into the riding arena the donkeys were very quiet, seeming to sense their need to remain quiet and still in readiness for their riders. One of the smaller donkeys, named Norman, waited patiently as I helped Jamie stretch out his legs, pulling each one in turn to loosen the tendons and ligaments; this took two of us using a handling belt to support him as well. I'd never seen him as happy as when the staff strapped on his safety helmet and sat him on Norman's back! 'Norman's my favourite,' Jamie said on the way home. 'Donkeys tomorrow?' From then on a day didn't go by when we didn't hear 'Donkeys tomorrow?' and whenever we attend the Centre he always asks, 'Is Norman here today?'

It's an incredible achievement for Jamie to even sit on a donkey, and I can't thank the EST staff enough. Riding has helped to increase the strength in his legs and exercises the muscles in his thighs and upper body. Every day he's getting stronger and can now stand, with support, to put on his coat. The doctors still don't know if he'll ever be able to walk, but that hasn't stopped him being a happy little boy.

Jamie went into a manual wheelchair on his fifth birthday. At the EST Summer Fair in June 2009 he was awarded a special trophy for being so cheerful – he was so proud! His confidence and spirit have had such a boost since he started visiting EST, and it's all down to the adorable donkeys. Jamie is seven years old now, and we are still attending the Saturday Club once a month for him to see and ride Norman.'

I was delighted to hand Jamie his cup for cheerfulness

ABOVE RIGHT *Jonah with one of his donkey friends*

Jonah

In Autumn 2009 Jonah's mother, Jacqueline, was given a list of activities for children with disabilities. One of these available was free donkey-riding therapy at the Birmingham Centre of the Elisabeth Svendsen Trust for Children and Donkeys (EST).

Jacqueline started bringing Jonah to the Centre every week and has seen a vast improvement in her son's abilities since he began riding donkeys. She told me:

'At first Jonah was scared of the donkeys, but after just three visits he overcame his fear and now absolutely adores them; it's the highlight of his week. The donkey riding has made a real difference to his muscle tone and balance so he doesn't fall over as much any more.'

DONKEYS

Kelly

Kelly is a grey mare, born in 1992, who was taken into The Donkey Sanctuary's care in 1997. She came from a loving and caring home in Scotland, but her owner felt she was getting too old to cope with such a young and energetic donkey. Kelly is a very pretty mare with a black shoulder cross and white legs.

After spending two years at the Sanctuary staff realised that she would be perfect for working with disadvantaged children, and she joined the team of donkeys chosen to work at the EST Centre in Leeds.

Although Kelly is a very contented donkey, she can be a bit greedy at feeding time. Not only has she managed to get her head stuck in a bucket on several occasions but recently, in her haste to get to the food, she managed to knock a wheelbarrow over and get the scoop shovel hooked over her neck. This didn't deter her in any way – she still managed to get to the carrots and ginger biscuits before the other donkeys – and with the shovel still attached!

Kelly

Kitty

Kitty was a thirty-one year old mare who came into the care of the Irish Donkey Sanctuary in October 2005 from Kanturk, County Cork as a result of a complaint case. Pat McGrath, the Welfare Officer who looked after the situation said it was the worst case of abuse he had ever seen. Her feet were

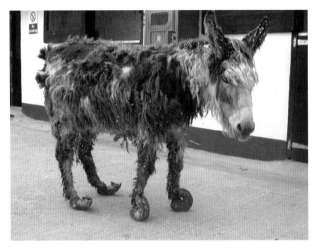

Kitty was in an appalling state when she came into care

overgrown to such an extent that they were curling upwards like Persian slippers and her coat was completely matted, with lice and sores all over her body. It was important to get her signed over to the Sanctuary as soon as possible so she could receive treatment.

Kitty was given intensive care; her feet were pared, she was deloused and her body sores were treated, and it was hoped that she would make a good recovery. However this was not to be and, due to cronic laminitis, Kitty was put to sleep in February 2006. It is believed that Kitty had the best five months of her life at the Sanctuary.

Kope

Kope's owner, Lemma Tulu, from Ganda Gorba in the Ada region of Ethiopia brought a seriously ill and pregnant Kope to the Donkey Sanctuary's donkey hospital in Debre Zeit. He knew about the hospital because one of its mobile teams visits his village on a regular basis to de-worm donkeys, treat their injuries and provide general advice.

Lemma and his family were very concerned at Kope's condition – she was becoming stiff legged and finding it difficult to eat. They couldn't afford to lose her, as she helped with everything from collecting their drinking water to transporting their goods to market to sell every day. Her unborn foal was valuable to them as well – it would cost at least a month's wages to buy another donkey. They knew their only chance was to walk Kope seven kilometres (over four miles) to the hospital to receive treatment. At the clinic she was immediately seen to be suffering from tetanus and admitted to the hospital. Just like in people, tetanus is a distressing disease for donkeys which affects the nervous system and can eventually paralyse and kill the animal.

Our veterinary team put in place an intensive veterinary care programme to help keep Kope alive. She was given tetanus anti-toxin, penicillin and other supportive drugs; and put on a drip because she was having trouble drinking; and she was encouraged to eat some soft mash to stop her starving. Tetanus makes donkeys over-sensitive to everything so the treatment included keeping her in the dark and filling her long, sad ears with cotton wool.

After two weeks of intensive nursing Kope was doing better than expected, but then she started to foal, and the risk of losing her life became a real threat once again. As Dr Bojia, our Country Representative in Ethiopia explained, her muscles were still partly paralysed by the toxins and so might not be able to relax enough for her to give birth properly. He was very concerned for Kope's

Kope with her foal, Obsa

safety. However with gentle care and patience they were able to help deliver a healthy little foal.

Kope seems to have defied all odds. Almost five weeks later she had made such great improvements that she was back at work for her owner, with her new foal, Obsa, by her side.

DONKEY FACTS, PEOPLE AND PLACES

Kenya – our work there

Our work in mainland Kenya began in 1994 when we donated funds for donkey treatments to the Kenya Society for the Protection and Care of Animals (KSPCA). By 2004 both organisations had agreed to a partnership arrangement which saw The Donkey Sanctuary establishing a base and harness workshop in the KSPCA's headquarters at Karen near Nairobi and setting up a 'donkey account' to pay for donkey treatments by the KSPCA's mobile clinics. We have treatment facilities at the KSPCA and three mobile teams of vet, harness maker and education or extension officer. These teams spend up to two weeks at a time out on the road, visiting clusters of donkey-owning communities in many different districts of Kenya. Some of these districts are relatively close to Nairobi; others are up to 400 km (250 miles) away and take several hours to reach.

Two education officers carry out separate school visits, and a harness field officer visits areas identified by the vets which have particular harness problems. In future the veterinary, harness and education work will be more closely integrated.

Donkey Sanctuary vet Solomon treating a neck wound caused by poor harness
Photograph courtesy of Tracy Brand

BELOW *A donkey cart in Kenya. Note that the donkey on the right is struggling with an old leg injury, a fracture which has healed without being set properly*

'Best in Show'

The island of Lamu lies just off the Kenyan coast in the Indian Ocean. Lamu Town, with its lovely old multi-story courtyard houses built around a network of narrow alleys, was built as a trading port in the 1700s. The donkeys will have been there at least as long. Visitors who have known Lamu over the twenty-three years we have been working there say how much better the donkeys look now. The Donkey Sanctuary opened a small Sanctuary in 1987 and has been working hard to improve conditions for more than two thousand donkeys that live there. The Sanctuary, on the sea front, is a place of refuge for donkeys recovering after treatment until they are well enough to return to work and we now also have a small inland farm where orphan foals are raised.

Since 1987, the Fourth of July is a special day on the island – nominated by me as 'Independence Day for the Donkeys' – the day of the annual best donkey competition! Each year owners bring their donkeys from all around Lamu Town to win this coveted accolade. The winning donkey has to be in good condition with good harness – but most important it has to be relaxed and comfortable with its owner.

The prize for 'Best in Show' 2010 was awarded to Abdala Hamid for his donkey, Cheusi. After the competition, Abdala was given a rosette and small prize in a presentation ceremony in front of an appreciative crowd. Abdala said he enjoys taking care of Cheusi and is proud to have won the competition particularly as he bought her after seeing that she was in a poor condition and needed a new owner to look after her. Abdalla was also drawn to Cheusi because of her unusual colour which means he will always be able to recognise her.

At the donkey competition

The African Mama

I'm getting old and losing my sight
And it's always hot in my hut at night.
In fact I can't see very much at all
And I have to be careful that I don't fall.

If you close your eyes you'll be like me
Please try now, then I'll have company.
It's amazing how we can shut out light,
Turn a wonderful day into darkest night.

My donkey shows me the way to town
I hold onto her collar, she won't let me down.
I've managed to balance some corn on her back
But I'm not sure I've properly tied on the sack.

Disaster strikes as we walk on the road
I hear the noise as she loses her load.
I try hard to see, but the lorries raise dust
And I'm so very frightened, but find it I must.

I feel a touch, a hand on my back
'Here, let me help you, I'll pick up your sack.
Just move here with me to the side of the road,
I'll help your donkey and refix your load'.

'Your poor donkey's thin and covered in sores
Does she belong to you – is she yours?'
It's the kindest voice I've heard for years
And suddenly my eyes are just filling with tears.

As if in a dream I'm helped in a van
My donkey led in by the very kind man.
He is talking so gently, and giving her feed
And now he is asking *me* what I need.

A miracle has happened for donkey and me
He's arranged for a doctor to help me to see.
They've lent me a donkey until mine is strong
And they help working donkeys all the day long.

My life began changing from that very day
And now I can see, as I kneel and I pray,
and thank God for the wonderful gift of sight
For seeing the daylight instead of the night.

Taken from Not Just Donkeys
by Dr Elisabeth D Svendsen and reproduced by
kind permission of Whittet Books Ltd

DONKEYS

Laurel and Hardy

The names inspire thoughts of fun and laughter, but not in this case. These two little donkeys and a pony called Tim had been shut in a filthy stable for at least six months. Molly Lloyd, Regional Welfare Officer responsible for her team of Area Welfare Officers, led the rescue. It began when an anonymous member of the public made her aware of the situation. Molly was shocked and distressed at the condition of the animals. They were extremely thin, had lice and their feet were painfully long.

The local police located the owner of the animals, who apparently did visit them every twenty-four hours to give them some food and water. Despite this Laurel, Hardy and Tim had not been able to leave the stable at any time. Their bedding was soaked in urine and faeces and the food they were being given was woefully inadequate. They were signed over to The Donkey Sanctuary later the same day and taken to the safety of the Derbyshire Centre, near Buxton to receive intensive care and permanent protection.

The Centre is used extensively as a perfect resting place for rescued donkeys to recover before continuing their journey from northern areas of the UK down to Devon. A full veterinary check was carried out and the farrier began remedial work on their feet. Chris Pile, manager of the Centre, told me, 'It's going to take a great deal of time and effort to bring them back to full health, but that's what The Donkey Sanctuary is here for'.

After six months at the Centre, Laurel, Hardy and Tim were brought down to the Sanctuary. Also with them was Tim's new friend, Gypsy. Of course they had to spend their first six weeks in our New Arrivals Unit.

The Sanctuary's Publicity Officer, Dawn Vincent, had been especially interested in the group from the day of their rescue, particularly as the programme-makers of BBC Television's 'Animals 24/7' had showed an interest and were filming their progress. As she told me:

'Watching them come off the lorry was really thrilling. They looked brilliant, thanks to the incredible work the staff at the Derbyshire Centre had done to bring the donkeys and Tim back to the handsome, healthy animals they deserve to be. I was lucky enough to watch as Laurel and Hardy explored their new home. Hardy was quite scared at first and would not leave Laurel's side; it made me realise that these two donkeys have a very strong bond. The next day, I returned to see them being turned out into their new paddock, which is rather large!

It was a magical moment when the gate was opened. They both ran to the middle of the field, turned around and stood proud, as if to stake their territory! They puffed out their chests and stood firmly with their ears forward. It was a far cry from their behaviour when we first rescued them. Then Hardy realised there were other donkeys in the neighbouring fields and began braying happily, which then set off all the other donkeys!'

Laurel and Hardy when they were rescued

ABOVE RIGHT *Laurel and Hardy today*

Laz

At fifty years old Laz is currently the oldest donkey at The Donkey Sanctuary. He came into care in 2000 and was the 8,209th donkey to pass through the Sanctuary's doors. He now lives at Woods Farm, where he enjoys a peaceful life surrounded by his friends. He can no longer eat hay, as he's lost some of his teeth, so he has to be given special soft food.

Although Laz is elderly he doesn't act his age as, particularly in the spring, he loves chasing the ladies around! Perhaps this is what keeps him fit!

Laz, currently the oldest donkey at The Donkey Sanctuary

León

León belongs to a breed of miniature donkeys that were rescued from Naples Zoo when it went into receivership in 2004. He shares his paddock at El Refugio del Burrito in Spain with a group of six other miniature donkeys. He can often be seen playfully running around with them. His cute looks and his boisterous antics have made him a favourite among staff and visitors alike.

León is always popular with visitors (he is one of El Refugio's donkey available under the Adoption Scheme), and is quite mischievous despite his small stature. He and his friends love using the feed bowls to play tug of war!

Little Vijay

Little Vijay is a brown gelding with a distinct cross on his back and a white belly. His mother, Rosemary, and her daughter had been relinquished to the Irish Donkey Sanctuary in County Cork as their elderly owner could no longer cope. Some months later they were brought over to the UK where, on 24th April 1994, Rosemary gave birth to a colt foal, the 6,079th to be in the Sanctuary's care. I decided to name him 'Little Vijay' in recognition of Dr Vijay Varma, a vet who helped donkeys in Kenya before The Donkey Sanctuary began work there.

Early in 2000 Little Vijay joined the team of donkeys at EST Sidmouth and his quiet reliable nature has shone through ever since. He is an excellent confidence-booster to the children who attend, particularly on their first ride,

León

and will stand very still whilst being stroked and groomed. He is also a member of the Adoption Scheme and consequently receives many visitors.

Although Little Vijay usually works in the arena, in December 2009 he was called upon to visit Little Bridge Children's Hospice in North Devon. A carol service was being held there and they asked if EST could bring along a gentle, well-behaved donkey which, of course, Little Vijay is! He behaved beautifully during the service, after which he went around to meet the sick children. He certainly brought joy to everyone's faces and helped create a magical evening to remember.

Lonnie

Lonnie had been taken in by The Donkey Sanctuary (Cyprus)'s former owners. He is so typical of a Cypriot donkey – dark brown, big and strong. He came into the Sanctuary in 2004 from a small village called Alona high up in the Troodos Mountains. His owner's wife had unfortunately died and he was not able to look after a rather boisterous donkey. The journey to collect Lonnie was a little treacherous as there was still quite a lot of snow on the mountains and sheer drops at the edge of the track. Although Lonnie had never been in a horse trailer before he was the perfect traveller.

Not long after arriving at the Sanctuary he became best friends with one of the other donkeys called Olive who can often be seen following him around. Still a cheeky chap, he is extremely nosy and definitely enjoys his cuddles, which made him an ideal candidate for the Cyprus Sanctuary's Adoption Scheme.

TOP PHOTO *Little Vijay*

LOWER PHOTO *Lonnie*

Loppy

It was a very quiet and worried vet who phoned me one day in early June 2004. A few days earlier we had received a report from an RSPCA Inspector, and I was aware that we might have to collect a donkey urgently at a moment's notice. So it wasn't a total surprise to receive the request to go and see the new arrival.

At the time, part of the New Arrivals Unit was closed because of a viral infection, so we'd had to make special arrangements to put the donkey in a different area within the isolation facilities. Loppy, a stallion, was in a poor condition and, when I arrived at the Isolation Unit, concerned staff were looking at him in horror. He was so thin that his ribs were showing, his hooves were long, he had scarred ears (with the tips missing) and an awful festering wound on his neck, which was probably the result of being attacked by other stallions prior to his rescue. He was very nervous and watched me from the corner of his eye as I approached him gently with a bucket of grass, carrots and apples. I'm sure he would have eaten the lot if I'd let him! Whilst he was feeding, I was able to stroke him gently and the vet took the opportunity to have a quick look at the nasty wound.

All the donkeys that come into our care are allowed at least twenty-four hours to settle down after the stress of leaving familiar surroundings and undertaking the journey. Loppy was, therefore, left in a stable of deeply bedded straw with fresh water. It wasn't long before his body language changed from utter despondency to a cautionary 'pricking up' of ears as he realised that his luck had changed.

I popped in to see Loppy after dark. He was lying down, relaxing and enjoying this newly found comfort, but he lifted his head and looked right at me. I'm sure that, in the glow of the yellow heat lamp I saw him nod, as if to say 'thank you'.

The next few days were touch and go for Loppy. Dung samples revealed massive parasitic infestation, including liver fluke and lungworm, and he was severely malnourished. However patience and love saved the day.

Loppy has one ear longer than the other!

Lorcan

Lorcan's plight was first reported to the ISPCA in Galway, who then contacted The Donkey Sanctuary in Ireland. Our Welfare Officer Patricia Daly took him to her livery base before transporting him to the Sanctuary in County Cork. She named him Lorcan after her grandson.

Lorcan, a lovely brown gelding with a white face, was only a year old. He was terribly thin when he arrived, with a body condition score of 1. His ears were flopped over due to an injury at their base. This had occurred when he had been chased by youths and had run into a barbed wire fence; the wire had nearly ripped both his ears off.

At first he was very wary of people and only Helen, the veterinary nurse, could get him to come to her, but he has recovered very well and now loves the attention he receives from visitors and staff alike. He has been one of the Irish Sanctuary's adoption donkeys since the scheme started in 2001.

Lorcan is especially fond of ginger nut biscuits; who could resist giving him an extra helping as he put his head on your shoulder and looks up with those big brown eyes? He tries this with staff and visitors alike!

Lorcan's ears are an endearing feature

Several months ago the lady that reported Lorcan to the ISPCA came to visit him. She recognised him from his adoption photo at the riding school her daughter attends. She was delighted to meet him again fifteen years later and to see him looking so well and happy.

Lorraine

Lorraine

Lorraine had been taken in by The Donkey Sanctuary (Cyprus)'s former owners. She had lived in a small village not too far from the Sanctuary and was relinquished into our care in 2002 aged twelve years. She had several severe wounds which were promptly treated and fortunately healed very well.

Despite her ordeal Lorraine is a very kind and gentle donkey with a wonderful temperament – a real lady. The only problem is her weight, so she is frequently on the Sanctuary's weight watchers programme! She loves being made a fuss of and taken for a walk, which invariably presents a good opportunity to have a sneaky nibble of something tasty on the way! She is a member of the Cyprus Donkey Sanctuary's Adoption Scheme.

Lucky and Lola

Following is the story of Lucky and her foal which was sent to me by Dr Ramesh Kumar, leader of our project in Ahmedabad in India.

'Our office in Ahmedabad received a phone call regarding a mare in severe distress. The gentleman who called us was a government official working in the electricity department in a village near the city of Gandhinagar. He contacted an animal welfare organisation in Ahmedabad, who in turn gave him our phone number. He reported that the mare was roaming the village, with severe wounds on the back of her thigh, which were maggot-infested, and the village dogs were chasing her around. The government official said that, although he wasn't sure, he thought the donkey might be pregnant.

The mobile team immediately left to attend the call. The village was about 45 km away. After searching the village for some time the mare was spotted near a pond. It was evident, even from a distance, that she was heavily in foal. On closer examination, she had three wounds from which blood was oozing. One of the wounds was very deep, with extensive tissue damage, including part of the vulva. Some cruel human being had inflicted the wounds using a sharp object, because he had found her grazing in his field. I really felt very sad to see the full-term mare with such wounds and in severe distress. I felt ashamed of the person who had done this, but very proud of the kind-hearted officer who had called us for help. We loaded the mare carefully into the ambulance and drove the vehicle very slowly to reach our clinic in Charodi.

On arrival at the clinic we named her Lucky. She was rested for a while, and given food and water. Her wounds were cleaned, the maggots were removed and dressings were applied.

It was bit worrying to think that Lucky might have difficulty in foaling and might even require a caesarean section because of the nature, position and extent of the damage. Hoping for the best we started the treatment. Days went by, with loving, expert care and attention her wounds were healing well.

After three weeks, one fine morning I received a call from the dresser at the clinic who told me that Lucky had given birth to a beautiful filly foal. I was very pleased to see when I examined them that she was fine and the foal was healthy and normal. It was wonderful to see how protective she was of her beautiful daughter. The foal deserves the love, care and protection of her mother because of the amount of pain and stress she underwent during her pregnancy. I just stood there for a moment admiring the motherly instinct. Like me, all the staff were very happy for Lucky and her foal, who we named Lola.'

Lucky with her foal, Lola

Lucky Lady

In the early days, running a hotel proved a great advantage for the welfare of donkeys. Visitors seeing them in the field made enquiries and were almost always interested, contributing funds too. Information began to come in as to where donkeys were in distress and an urgent call came one boiling hot August day from a guest at the hotel who was visiting a local resort. 'Mrs Svendsen, I do wish you could come – this poor little donkey has been giving rides all day and has collapsed. They've left it at the side of the beach under a sack but it's still alive.' Niels was away so I jumped in my car and drove off. When I got to the beach the hotel guest was waiting anxiously. 'They've got it in that lorry which is just leaving,' she said. I followed the lorry and after a few miles it arrived at a rough field. It was met by a man, obviously the owner, who started talking to the driver. He was large and rough. Together they climbed into the back of the lorry. I peered in.

'Excuse me, is that your donkey?' I asked. A stream of bad language emerged to the effect that she was a lazy bag and had ruined his day's trade. 'Can I have a look at her please?' 'No, clear off, she'll be all right after a rest. Those buggers just need a clout on the head and then they behave. I should have been on the beach myself and not let that young girl have them…' 'Get up,' he yelled at the donkey and brandished a large stick, striking her on the quarters. I felt sick.

'I'll buy her if you like,' I said. 'She's not much use to you – what do you want for her?' 'She'll be all right when she's had a taste of this,' he said, and struck her again. 'If you hit her again I'll kill you.' It stopped him; he laughed. I suppose it was an idle threat but I have never been able to accept violence towards defenceless creatures. 'I'll sell her for forty pounds,' he said. 'I'll give you thirty-five pounds delivered to the Salston Hotel.' He lifted his stick again. 'All right, forty pounds, but delivered.' My heart was thumping but the donkey had lifted her head and was looking at me. He climbed out of the lorry. 'Where's the cash then?' I made out a cheque and scribbled a receipt for him to sign. The driver set off for Ottery St Mary and as the lorry left I turned to the man and said, 'I'll tell the RSPCA about this and if ever there's a repeat of such bad treatment I will be back.'

I passed the lorry and led it home. Niels had since arrived. He was concerned to see my tear-stained face, but as always he understood and helped to gently unload the donkey. The vet hurried out and once again he shook his head. 'She's about forty-five years old and she's had a heart attack. I'll do my best, but …'

The old lady fought for her life – she really fought! We spoon-fed her, she had injections twice a day – and of course hot bran mash with black treacle which she was able to enjoy. Three days later she was standing up in the yard. The guest who had rescued her came to have a look. 'She really is a lucky lady now,' she said, and Lucky Lady she became. She improved steadily but was not really able to hold her own with the other donkeys. At this time Niels' stepfather, Svend Iversen, was living on his own in Exeter and he had a beautiful orchard. He offered to give Lucky Lady a home until she was able to fend for herself. As space was a big problem this seemed ideal and an extremely close relationship built up between the two. As he obviously never carried a stick or mistreated her in any way Lucky Lady began to regain her confidence in human beings – and, indeed, to get a bit of her own back. Svend had to be very careful only to bring the very best hay into the field – any poor quality material was inspected immediately and, before he had time to get to the gate she would trot in front of him, turn round and give him a not too gentle kick, just to let him know he was not fully appreciated! After three years of this love-hate relationship the orchard was sold and Lucky Lady returned to us. The very sad day came when it was kinder to put her to sleep, a decision we have to take when we feel a donkey no longer has any quality of life.

Lucky Lady

DONKEY FACTS, PEOPLE AND PLACES

Lectures

In the very early days, when I was getting The Donkey Sanctuary going I was frequently asked to speak at such events as WI meetings, Probus Clubs, Masonic functions and men's forums – Order of the Buffalo, the Lions, Men of Trees and Rotary. People were always interested in the progress of the Sanctuary and donated generously at the end of the lectures. Many groups came to visit us and became firm supporters at a time when they were desperately needed. Television and radio were often pressing me to give interviews, and it became part of the job.

In 1985 I received the first of many invitations to give a paper at the World Association for the Advancement of Veterinary Parasitology (WAAVP) Conference. These Conferences are held bi-annually in different parts of the world each time, and this one was to be in Rio de Janeiro. I spent a long time writing my paper and speaking to various people to get as many tips as I could.

A few months previously I had attended a meeting in Newmarket with regard to the British Equine Veterinary Association's projects for the coming years. Various papers had been given and, as far as I could see, most of these were concerned with racehorses or eventing and how to improve performance – there were also papers on multiple births and other projects I personally felt to be intrusive and which I didn't particularly like. As I'd been asked to represent welfare groups I stood up and made my comments clearly, pointing out that I was sure the general public would be willing to subscribe to BEVA if something practical was done with regard to horses being injured in racing and jumping. I often felt that having to shoot a horse because it had a broken leg was unnecessary, as in some cases I was quite sure the horse could carry on to live a happy life although, of course, he would no longer be commercially viable. I was given the cold shoulder at lunch time, and was sitting alone at a table when a very nice gentleman asked if he could join me. We began chatting and I learned that he would be giving a paper at the Conference in Rio too. I was told later that the gentleman was Lawson Soulsby (now Lord Soulsby of Swaffham Prior), one of the world's foremost experts on parasitology.

On arrival at the hotel in Rio I went down to dinner and decided to have a glass of wine with my meal. Glancing through the list I was amazed to see that the Moet et Chandon champagne was priced at the equivalent of £4.80 a bottle. I couldn't believe this was right, as even a bottle of Beaujolais was £30! Just for fun I ordered a bottle of champagne. To my surprise the most beautiful bottle arrived – a very early vintage and in absolute perfect drinking condition. I managed two glasses, replaced the cork and bore the remainder away to my room. The next day the other delegates arrived, and one of the first people to come and greet me was Lawson and his charming wife, Annette. I said to them, 'why don't you come for a little party this evening by the pool?' and they immediately agreed, as did several other colleagues I invited. I went inside and ordered four bottles of champagne, which duly arrived on the table and caused a great impression on everyone present. I paid cash, so that there could be no dispute at a later date if we found it had been wrongly charged. How wise I was! After that lovely party Lawson invited us all to join them a few days later. He laughed when I looked surprised that there was only one bottle of champagne on the table. He said, 'Betty, I think they've found the error of their ways – the champagne should have been priced at £48!' To this day we often joke about our first champagne party in Rio de Janeiro.

I was presenting my paper on the last day of the Conference and to prepare myself and settle my nerves I visited the room that had been allocated to the equine lectures, making myself feel comfortable at the podium and practising my talk to what I knew, because of the size of the room, could not be more than a maximum of a hundred people. During the Conference plenary lectures were given in the enormous auditorium which could seat over a thousand delegates. Each paper was automatically translated into four different languages and of course the speakers were all fluent and practised. After a sleepless night I arrived to give my paper the next morning and was surprised to find the lecture room completely empty and some of the chairs removed. My first thought was that at least I'll only have a very small audience, but then I was told there had been a change of venue – I'd been put in the main auditorium!

I was terrified! The room was over half full, which meant that I had an audience of over five hundred vets and veterinary parasitologists – all of them qualified and experts in their field. I knew I had to make an impact at the beginning, as obviously a paper on donkeys, probably the first in the world to be given on this particular species, was of no obvious interest to most of them. So I started off by asking them all a question. I said, 'I'm not a qualified vet, and I do thank you for giving your time to listen to me today, but I want to ask you two questions. The first one is: can anyone here tell me the average temperature of a donkey?' There was silence, so I continued, 'Would you think it's the same as a horse, and would you treat the donkeys the same as a horse? Those of you who think this please raise your hands.' Almost immediately nearly every person in the hall raised his hand, and I was able to say to them, 'well, if you are treating a donkey with the average temperature of a horse, that donkey is probably going to die.' The average temperature of the donkey is 98.8° – slightly above that of a human, and that of the horse is 101°, and the fact that no research into the donkey has previously been done to even tell veterinary surgeons this most essential basic need to treat the species gave me the courage to continue.

After I'd finished I was inundated with questions from many of the delegates and I was asked if I would give another paper the following year in Atlanta, Georgia at the Conference of the American Veterinary Medical Association/American Association of Veterinary Parasitologists. I readily agreed, as I knew the more we could spread the word to the professional people the more hope donkeys were going to have in the future.

It was very hot in Atlanta; the temperature was nearly 100°, but fortunately the Conference was held in an air-conditioned hall. There was a very large audience of American vets, lecturers, students and representatives of the commercial organisations associated with animal feedstuff and nutrition. Professor Max Murray of the University of Glasgow gave a great opening lecture and then it was my turn. It never ceased to amaze me that little or nothing was known about donkeys within the veterinary profession, yet in my opinion donkeys have helped man more than any other animal in the world. Where would the poorest people in the developing world be without their donkey to help with carrying such necessities as water, building materials and goods to and from the markets? In addition they were often used for ploughing when oxen were not available or had died because of the drought conditions. Donkeys have proved themselves able to exist with only small amounts of water – even more so than camels. The vets were fascinated with what I had to say and I received many promises of help. It was the donkey's day!

Perhaps the most interesting Conference for cultural reasons was held in East Berlin in 1989. The Berlin Wall was still in place and we had special guards all the time. The people looked very impoverished and I was surprised to find the hotel shop selling luxuries – apparently for guests only; locals were not allowed to see them!

Whilst there I visited Berlin Zoo with Bill Jordan, one of the Sanctuary's Trustees at the time. Bill is a qualified vet and had been doing the 'donkey work' with me around the world for several years. To my surprise I found a substantial cage in which were four large Poitou donkeys! We were being escorted by two security guards and the owner of the zoo. I asked if I could go in.

'Oh no,' he said. 'These are very dangerous animals.' Succumbing to my powers of persuasion the owner reluctantly opened the door and I walked in. As you may know, Poitou donkeys are the gentlest, friendliest animals. I called them the shire horse of the donkey world. They are as large as a horse and have gigantic ears. To the keeper's amazement the largest donkey came straight up to me and leaned his great head on my shoulder! Soon all four were surrounding Bill and me, and the keeper decided with a little help from us that perhaps instead of being in a cage they could be in a pen with wooden bars so that they could see the public!

In 1993 the WAAVP Conference was hosted by Cambridge in the UK. Because of the interest we had attracted in Rio we were invited to run a workshop within the Conference proceedings. I had the honour of chairing it, which was a new experience for me. It was very well attended and both Andrew Trawford, our Director of Veterinary Services, and Don Bliss, the American Parasitologist I had been working with in Greece, helped in the preparation and gave excellent papers. Donkeys at last were being giving serious attention.

In 1997 the event was in Sun City in South Africa. What an amazing venue! It was like a small Las Vegas and it was lucky that the majority of us were able to concentrate on the programme, as temptation awaited us on the way to and from lectures! Professor Aline de Aluja, our team leader in Mexico and an extremely knowledgeable person was giving two lectures – one for us on our donkey project in Mexico where she organised our team of vets, and one for the University of Mexico's Veterinary Faculty (UNAM) on the transmission of parasites from pigs to humans! This is known as zoonosis. She was lecturing in a different part of the Conference Hall from me, and the questions at the end of my lecture made me late for Aline's lecture. As I approached the room I was surprised to see a young man slumped on the floor outside the door. His face was covered in sweat and was completely green! 'Are you OK?' I enquired. 'No,' came the reply. 'I'm a fourth year veterinary student at the university here and I thought I could stand anything. I'm here to work the slides and this Mexican Professor is in the middle of her lecture – her slides are showing people sitting on toilets made with two planks over a hole. Underneath are masses of pigs fighting over what is dropping down. Then it shows people eating the pigs! I can't do it any more!' Fortunately for me, by the time I fetched help for the now-vomiting student the lecture had finished.

Perhaps my biggest honour was to be asked to open the BEVA (British Equine Veterinary Association) Congress in Glasgow in September 2002. The big day arrived and I was introduced by the organiser, Professor Sandy Love, to the 1,400-strong delegates. I started off by saying, 'Good morning everybody,' to which I got absolutely no response! I tried again. 'Come along ladies and gentlemen! This is a difficult moment for me and I need your help. *Good morning* ladies and gentlemen!' A roar of 'good mornings' came back at me and, from that moment on, as I advised them of The Donkey Sanctuary's work, I had their full attention. Sandy couldn't have been more delighted as he helped me down from the podium, thanking me for doing such a good job on their behalf.

Fundraising has always been an important part of my job, and in 2003 I was asked to give a lecture at a Charities Aid Foundation Conference in London. This was a complete change from my usual veterinary talks and I took along my granddaughter, Dawn Vincent, to help me with a PowerPoint presentation, entitled 'Keeping our Heads above Water'.

Today, as Founder of The Donkey Sanctuary, I often receive invitations to speak at functions but unfortunately as I am now in

Opening the BEVA Congress in September 2002

my 80s and following two minor strokes, I have to decline. The main exception is during Donkey Week each year, when I feel able to rise to the occasion. I'm delighted to welcome them all and do my best to make them feel happy and at home. My talk always includes one of 'mother's little jokes'!

My welcome to 'Donkey Weekers'. I always stand at the top of the steps leading from the offices down to our main yard, hence my talk is now known as my 'Sermon on the Mount'!

Being outperformed!

I first encountered Betty Svendsen, one of the most remarkable women I have ever known, at the Conference of the American Veterinary Medical Association/American Association of Veterinary Parasitologists held in Atlanta in 1986. I had been invited to give a keynote address on Genetic Resistance of Ruminants to Parasites. This was a subject I felt strongly about and at the end of my paper the audience response seemed very positive.

There were several papers in this session, one of which was presented by Betty. She spoke passionately about the wisdom of donkeys, their incredible work ethic and their physiological strength: they were a distinct species and were not small horses. I found it a spellbinding presentation. At the end of the session, I saw a flood of delegates coming towards me at the front of the conference hall and assumed it was to congratulate me on my delivery. I awaited their plaudits and I was therefore surprised that the crowd rushed passed me to the blonde lady just behind – Betty Svendsen! This was an audience reaction that I had never seen before or since. We all realised that we had witnessed a very extraordinary presentation, and I had to acknowledge that I was totally outperformed. What a remarkable lady!

Contributed by Professor Max Murray, Former Dean of the Faculty of Veterinary Medicine of the University of Glasgow

Lewis

Lewis was a senior student from Mill Ford School in Plymouth, who attended EST Ivybridge weekly for barn/stable management sessions. He has Down's Syndrome, and when he first started attending he was very immobile. He would sit in his wheelchair and his teachers would push him around, as he rarely wanted to get up and join in with the other students. He was quite stubborn, and did not want to interact with anyone other than a select few.

As time has passed we have seen a massive change in Lewis. The grooms included him in the sessions as much as possible – encouraging him to join in, communicate and have fun. Lewis started to get out of his wheelchair, walk around and throw the straw about the barn, having fun with his class mates. As he became more mobile, his confidence grew and he even started to become a real team leader within the group.

Lewis showed such big changes and made such an effort that we decided he should be awarded the 'St Francis Cup for Achievement' award at the 2010 Summer Fair. He was absolutely delighted! Even though he has now left Mill Ford School, he still comes back to see us and sometimes joins in with his old class for barn management.

Lewis is such a happy young man nowadays!

Liam

Liam first came to EST Manchester with the Portage Support Scheme (a national pre-school support service, for SEN and disabled children) when he was two and a half years old. At that time he had very little muscle tone and was not yet walking. Even in those early days riding the donkeys heightened his muscle tone and he took his first steps in the play area when waiting for his turn to ride. Liam has global developmental delay and is now eight years old. His whole family, including his younger brother Ben, who also has special needs, feel we are a huge part of their lives. Tracey, his mother, says that Liam is accepted at the Centre; it's a place where they can 'chill out' and although Liam continues to benefit in many ways, especially his core stability, she feels the social aspects are just as important as the riding. They have made close friends over the years, and during the holiday periods they arrange their rides so that both children and families can share the experience.

Liam loves it when his donkey trots around the arena

Tracey has nothing but praise for both staff and volunteers who have shown such patience with Liam. He is now more mature and all the family are able to see his face when he trots – a huge beaming smile which just says it all!

Lizzie

Lizzie has Down's Syndrome and regularly attends the EST Ivybridge Centre for riding therapy. She now attends Goosewell Primary School but more recently visited us from Downham Nursery, a special school in Plymstock. Both schools visit the centre weekly. Lizzie also comes along with her parents and brother, William, during Saturday/Holiday Clubs, and has celebrated three birthdays by holding her party at the Centre.

Lizzie was very shy when she first started coming to the Centre. She would constantly cling to her mother, Mel, would hardly talk or sign to us, and object to wearing a riding hat. She would start to cry and make a big fuss when mounting the donkeys and would always want mum by her side to support her.

As time went on staff noticed how much she was improving in all aspects. She started communicating with staff and volunteers by signing, and pointing out things she liked around the arena, like toys and posters. She was able to mount the donkeys with little fuss, and started stroking and even cuddling them.

Lizzie's confidence grew so much and she started to become quite independent – dashing about causing mischief, choosing and putting on her riding hat before the instructors could get the chance, and impatiently jumping about the ramp eager to mount the donkeys! Now she even tries to sneak in an extra ride – and succeeds on occasions! Lizzie is now able to ride with only staff and volunteers by her side, and waves happily to her mother as she rides by. She loves to play gymkhana games, which are very loud and fast paced – proving just how much her confidence has grown. Everyone is very fond of Lizzie and her brother; they are always smiling, full of fun and even cheeky at times! We always look forward to their visits.

Lizzie had achieved so much that, in 2010, she was awarded 'The Arran Sutton Cup for Growth in Self-Confidence and Esteem'. This award is presented annually during the Sumer Fair, and Lizzie is the third recipient of the trophy. Arran Sutton was one of our original volunteers and worked tirelessly, along with her husband Alan, on the mobile project – which operated for five years prior to the Centre being built. Sadly, Arran passed away in 2007, the day after the donkeys arrived at their new home in Ivybridge. Alan still works as a volunteer.

Lizzie being presented with her award by John Akers, EST's Chief Executive, at the EST Ivybridge Summer Fair 2010

On a mule you find
Two feet behind,
Two feet you find before.
You stand behind
Before you find,
What the two behind be for!

DONKEYS

Manolito and Sevillano

El Refugio del Burrito in Spain received a call from a lady in Frigiliana who had two donkeys and needed them to be rescued urgently. Because of the high level of rain over the previous few months the lady's house had collapsed. She had to be evacuated and her beloved donkeys had to leave as well.

Manolito and Sevillano were collected within the next few days. The track had collapsed due to the rain so it wasn't possible to reach them with the horsebox, so they had to be walked down from their paddock. After successfully loading them the journey was a bumpy ride out of the mountains and a terrifying experience due to the state of the flooded and mud-covered roads, but the driver, Trevor, kept calm and drove really well. Sevillano travelled the whole journey with his head over the partition holding on to his little friend Manolito, as if to reassure him.

Sadly Sevillano died a few months later and, as we were worried about Manolito developing hyperlipaemia following the loss of his friend, he was put with another donkey named Regalao. Regalao was chosen because he resembled Sevillano in so many ways – not just physically but his personality was very similar. They live at Doña Rosa, El Refugio's second farm in the Extremadura region.

Manolito

Mary (1)

Mary (1)

Mary is a brown jenny, born in 1992. In 2002 her owner sadly died and Mary, along with her daughter, Sarah, came into The Donkey Sanctuary's care.

Mary had been a much-loved pet, and she enjoys being groomed and stroked. She is calm and ladylike and, with her gentle and loving nature is ideal to work with children who attend the EST Centre in Manchester. It takes a special kind of donkey who can be ridden by special needs children one day and the next travel to a residential home. Mary is just the girl for the job! The charm of her soft dark brown coat and white muzzle ensures she gets lots of attention; we're often told that she is still a topic of conversation a week after her visit!

Mary (2)

Mary was discovered by our Welfare Officer, Marie McCormack, at a market in Northern Ireland in December 2009. She was in a terrible state, had a body score of just 1 – the poorest, thinnest condition a donkey can reach. She was suffering from rainscald on her ears and on her back, and had an infestation of worms, as well as neglected, painful hooves. To make matters worse, she had a foal by her side in an equally poor state and was in foal again.

Mary was so exhausted when she arrived at our holding base in County Tyrone that she couldn't stand up at all for the first three days. Her young foal, despite our best efforts, had suffered too much and sadly passed away.

Marie and her helper, Victor, spent three weeks providing Mary with round-the-clock care. They visited her three times throughout the night to

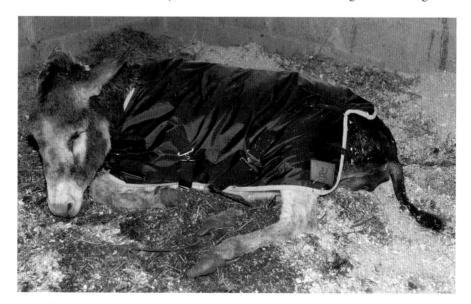

Mary (2) was very poorly when she first came into our care

make sure she was eating and give her much-needed vitamin boosters. They also had to lift her up to prevent 'bed sores' and to encourage her to get moving. Very sadly, she aborted her unborn foal halfway through her pregnancy, due to the severe neglect she had endured.

Since then Mary has been making a gradual recovery; she is gaining weight and improving in condition daily. She was very depressed after losing her foals, so when an abandoned foal, Owen, was rescued in early 2010 Mary was delighted to become his foster mother and the pair are now inseparable. She now has the strength to roll and canter in her field, kicking up her heels as she goes!

Merlin and Susie

Merlin and Susie came into The Donkey Sanctuary's care in 1996 following the death of their owner, Derek Tangye, the well-known author of the *Minack Chronicles*. Derek and his wife, Jeannie, lived a simple life on a Cornish cliff top and his books reflected their lives there, the most important part being caring for their donkeys.

The pair settled happily in New Barn at the Sanctuary, and enjoyed their 'star status' with the many visitors who came to see them. Merlin sadly died in 2005 but Susie spent a further five happy years at the Sanctuary before she too passed away.

Merlin and Susie were two of my favourites!

Mickos

Poor Mickos had been a stray in the Sugar Loaf mountain area south-west of Glengarriff in County Cork, Ireland, since his owner died eighteen years before. He had no shelter, and was surviving on titbits from passing hikers on

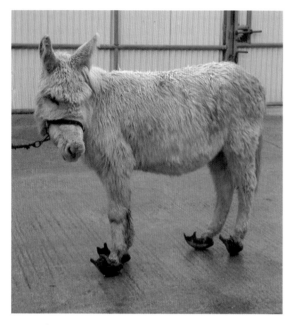

Mickos' hooves were in a terrible state on arrival at the Irish Sanctuary

the Kerry Way and whatever rough grazing he could find. However, a concerned hiker reported to our Irish Sanctuary in Liscarroll that Mickos had very overgrown hooves – they were long, turned upwards and split. He was also suffering from rainscald, a nasty skin condition suffered by donkeys when their skin gets excessively wet from standing in heavy, driving rain. Having located Mickos, Welfare Officer, Veronica Sheehan, immediately called a vet and the Gardai and, a phone call later, the lorry was sent to collect him.

Paddy Barrett, who was manager of the Sanctuary in Liscarroll at that time, was initially concerned about the damage to Mickos' hooves, but he steadily improved, thanks to farriery treatment, extra feeds at breakfast time, painkillers administered by way of a 'sandwich' (where the drug is hidden between slices of bread), as well as lots of expert, loving care and attention.

Micky (1)

Micky is a television star! In December 2009 the BBC television programme 'Animals 24:7' featured his relinquishment to The Donkey Sanctuary and his relocation to a new life in Devon.

Micky (1) the television star!

Micky had been living with another donkey that he was strongly bonded to but, after his friend died, he started showing physical signs of stress. His owners bravely decided that for the good of his health he should come and live with our donkeys.

After his period in the new arrivals unit Micky was relocated to Woods Farm. Although he has not yet found another donkey to bond with, he is getting on famously with his new friends, who all enjoy playing and running around in their paddock.

Micky (2)

Jenifer Tucker, the Sanctuary's Web Editor, was walking by the hospital paddocks when she noticed a donkey standing quite contentedly with a divot of grass in his mouth. She was intrigued and went to find out more him. She told me, 'Micky had been returned from a foster home after his foster owner's circumstances changed and, like all new arrivals, he spent his first six weeks in our New Arrivals unit. During this time, he made friends with a donkey called Freddie. Sadly, Freddie had then died so, to give him some company, Micky was put with two other donkeys, Merlin and Figaro.

When donkeys become friends they forge an incredibly strong bond and at the Sanctuary we always keep bonded donkeys together for the rest of their lives. So when, in September 2009, Merlin sustained an injury to one of his ears and needed veterinary care, he was taken into our veterinary hospital – and, of course, his best friends Figaro and Merlin joined him.

Micky (2) enjoying his favourite pastime!

Over the years, Micky has developed a habit of picking up a divot of grass and spending hours playing with it! We think that years ago he may have become bored and started looking for something to do, and this has now become a habit. He certainly appeared totally stress-free and relaxed that morning!'

Moses works at the EST Birmingham Centre and, when not helping the children he often looks for something to do. He surprised the staff one day by putting his head on Lorna's shoulder to examine the crossword she was doing ... '5 Across: six letters – 'Orange coloured vegetable, a donkey's favourite'!

Mossie

Our Sanctuary in Ireland is always overflowing. There are still many donkeys there and, due to the recession, more and more are either being abandoned or being sent in to us. Noel Carton, our Head of Operations in Ireland, was quite shocked to see a little donkey named Mossie, who had been abandoned. Mossie was in a terrible state; his hooves were severely overgrown and he was caked in thick mud and dung up as far as his chest.

Mossie on arrival

Mossie now enjoying life to the full

Mossie was X-rayed to establish the best way to tackle the appalling condition of his feet if, indeed, it was possible to do so. Fortunately it was decided to make an attempt to repair the damage and it seems we were just in time.

Despite his difficulties Mossie is a really friendly donkey. His treatment continues and he is enjoying lots of love and affection from our Irish staff. Just look at him now!

Mozart

Mozart, a twenty-five-year-old donkey, had lived with the same family for twenty-three of those years. As too often tragically happens, his owners gradually became too elderly to look after him and for the last two and a half years he had simply been left shut in a stable which was never mucked out and he was only occasionally given some hay. When the wife died, the husband found it difficult to visit the stable and Mozart rarely had food or, even worse, water. The husband then died, but fortunately they had a daughter who contacted us, as she felt she couldn't cope.

With great difficulty, as Mozart was terrified of humans, he was coaxed into our lorry and taken a short distance to our nearest holding base.

Our Welfare Officer, Shelagh Steel, was horrified to see his condition on his arrival. His feet were twisted and overgrown from standing on the filthy floor and he was crawling with lice. He was gently led into a stable, where he immediately went into a corner, cowering with fear when Shelagh tried to get near him. After the first day, during which he was able to get over the journey,

Mozart enjoyed two happy years at the Sanctuary

Shelagh let down the bars of the stable, but Mozart was too frightened to come out. Gradually over the next few days he became a little braver, so Shelagh tried putting him in a field with a very gentle, elderly donkey but Mozart was so frightened that he ran away! He was extremely emotionally disturbed.

Gradually he began to improve and was transferred to The Donkey Sanctuary. I nearly cried on his arrival, but he became much braver, venturing out into his paddock, even playing with the toys he was given – a bucket and a ball. Donkeys usually 'pair up' with another single donkey and make lifelong friends; Mozart, however, made two friends, Sootie and Minor, both single donkeys that had lost their partners. He became more friendly, coming up to the staff, especially at meal times, but as his special carer said, 'if you're not careful he can be a bit handy with his back legs!'

Sadly we lost him in 1999. He'd appeared to be in perfect health apart from a lump on his jaw and was in the process of being groomed when he suddenly dropped dead. It was a great shock to us all, but the post mortem revealed cancerous tumours on his lungs and kidneys. We were at least pleased that Mozart's end was swift and painless and that he'd had over two years' happiness and contentment at the Sanctuary.

DONKEY FACTS, PEOPLE AND PLACES

Mama Punda

I am known as Mama Punda in Kenya in recognition of my work in that country. It is translated as 'Mother of the Donkeys' and it is a name I am proud to be called!

Mama Punda – working with donkeys in Kenya

Memorial Day

Legacies make up a very large part of The Donkey Sanctuary's income and every legacy is recognised by an inscription on our Bequest Walls. In addition the charity has various types of Memorial Schemes. The Sanctuary is a beautiful and relaxing place, with many visitors returning time and time again to meander along the walks around the fields and, because of its peaceful atmosphere, it is natural for visiting supporters to ask for a dedication for a loved one or pet to be put in place. Alternatives are plaques in the Memorial Garden, trees and plaques on the Memory Walks, a Field of Dreams Fund or an entry in our Book of Remembrance.

The Donkey Sanctuary holds an annual Memorial Day in early October on or near the feast day of St Francis of Assisi, the Patron Saint of Animals, when we remember those people whose names are inscribed around the Sanctuary. Personal invitations are sent to their families with details of the service, which is held by the 'Sanctuary' vicar and followed by the blessing of memorials.

Reed crosses are placed on each memorial for the day and flowers can be organised on a supporter's behalf, which are put in place over the Memorial Day period.

BELOW *Flowers on memorial plaques in the Russell Garden*

Mexico – our work there

Having received many complaints from visitors to Mexico on the state of the donkeys there, in 1984 I decided to visit and meet up with Dr Aline de Aluja, a vet who worked for the Faculty of Veterinary Medicine at UNAM (the National Autonomous University of Mexico). I had met Dr Aline previously at one of the many Conferences I was attending in those days. I was accompanied by Bill Jordan, one of our Trustees at the time, and we received an enthusiastic response from the University and the Ministry of Agriculture, who agreed to co-operate on a joint project to help the donkeys in their country. We employed our own vet, Enrique Nunez, who came to the UK for a six-week training course, so that he could see our hospital and how we cared for donkeys here. He then returned to Mexico to work with the donkeys on our behalf. The Veterinary University agreed to do all the laboratory work free of charge and to assist with Enrique's salary.

We were appalled by the state of some of those poor donkeys in Mexico. Apart from suffering terribly from saddle galls and wounds, their main problem appeared to be parasites, and I was determined that our charity would try and help in whatever way it could. A worming programme led to the setting up, in 1988, of the first mobile unit travelling to villages around Mexico City.

On many of our visits to Mexico we were faced with horses that also had appalling wounds and worm burdens. We felt we had to help them as well, but as our charity restricted our work to donkeys and mules only, in 1990 we approached the International League for the Protection of Horses (ILPH) which is now World Horse Welfare. They agreed to join our teams and began paying half the costs so that horses could be treated too.

Today we have a mixed staff of veterinarians, farriers and education/extension officers based at the Faculty in Mexico City and at a field station in Veracruz state, by the Caribbean coast in the east of Mexico. We also use UNAM's veterinary facilities for treating donkeys, horses and mules, and training student vets in equine medicine.

The vets work in 'circuits' of communities. The locations visited are peri-urban (e.g. rubbish dumps) or rural communities, often spread across enormous geographical areas involving days of travel. Visits may take place weekly or six-monthly and involve veterinary treatments supported by educational talks or demonstrations. Recently we have started focusing our work, building up the training side and reducing the total amount of travel.

The community development and education work started with primary school visits only loosely tied to where the rest of the work was being carried out. Now it is moving towards a whole community approach, targeting places with serious welfare problems where this kind of intervention can make a real difference.

We also engage in advocacy and 'moral support' collaborations with other animal welfare organisations in other cities, and we have relationships with other veterinary faculties and with AMVEE (the Mexican Equine Veterinary Association).

Near Mexico City, whole families live on rubbish dump sites, picking out recyclable items from the huge piles of waste which they can sell for a few pesos. Donkeys, horses and mules are used to collect cartloads of rubbish from the city and bring it to the dumps. Our vets and farriers make regular visits treating harness sores and hoof problems and we have trained a local man to help adapt the harness.

We have been working at San Bernabe market since 1991 to try and improve the treatment of equines being sold for their meat value. Many are brought to the market with severe injuries and suffer greatly throughout the transportation, unloading and trading process, right up until the slaughter-house puts them out of their misery. We achieved representation on the market committee in order to push for change, and have managed to help provide better livestock pens with water troughs, along with loading and unloading ramps (animals often used to fracture their legs while being forced in and out of flat-bed trucks high off the ground). However there is a long way to go. Dr Aline has now secured funding from the Government for a market improvement plan that will unfold over the next two years. This is a very positive development and we look forward to seeing further progress.

As well as its routine work, the Veracruz project is leading the way in providing advice to outside organisations on all aspects of our work, most recently

A donkey working on a rubbish dump near Mexico City

Mexican mountain community donkeys

BELOW
Donkey Sanctuary farrier, Marco, demonstrating farriery techniques

co-ordinating the World Horse Welfare course in farriery. It is also spear-heading an 'equitarian' initiative with the American Association of Equine Practitioners (AAEP). All our staff within the university system give lectures on equine sciences.

Morocco – our work there

In Morocco, pack mules accompany groups of tourists on guided treks across the mountains, transporting their luggage and supplies. Thanks to a project funded by The Donkey Sanctuary, the welfare of the mules is now a key factor in the way the guides plan and conduct these expeditions.

The muleteer guides attend a year-long Mountain Leader Training pro-gramme at a national centre in Tabant, but in the past the programme included very little information on the health and welfare needs of their pack animals. In 2008 The Donkey Sanctuary was approached by a vet, Dr Glen Cousquer MRCVS, who had been researching the potential for using veterinary and education work to improve the welfare of pack mules. He wanted to develop a module within the Mountain Leader Training programme at Tabant which would teach the guides how to manage and handle the mules better, and give them basic first aid skills. The students would learn about nutrition and load-ing, and how to prevent common problems such as saddle sores and wounds, tethering injuries, and hoof and foot injuries caused by worn or loose shoes. Equipped with all this information, they would also be able to make sure the routes of their expeditions were not too arduous for the mules, and arrange stopping-places where the mules would have good access to food, water and shelter.

The Donkey Sanctuary funded the first week-long course on 'Pack Animal Care for Mountain Guides' at the end of March 2010. The students were given both theory and practical training, including hands-on work with mules. They were also given handouts on feeding, wound care and the training of mules, and the training centre's library was equipped with extra books on the subject. The course was well received and The Donkey Sanctuary is continuing to fund it in future years.

Muleteer guides on their training programme

Mules

The Romans were keen mule breeders; apparently emperors, popes, queens and noble ladies rode mules instead of horses, as they were considered to be special. Mules were used by the Roman army and in wartime, although they were never used as cavalry chargers as they have a high sense of self-preservation and would therefore refuse to run head first into danger! They were later used as pack animals to carry guns and supplies. It is said that mules were strapped to pallets and parachuted out of planes into war zones.

George Washington introduced a mule breeding programme to America after he was given a large Spanish jack by the King of Spain 1785, and today mules are hugely popular in America.

The Donkey Sanctuary has rescued a total of 159 mules and hinnies in the UK since it started, and currently there are 124 mules and hinnies in its care. A mule is a cross between a male donkey and a female horse or pony. A hinny is a cross between a female donkey and a male horse or pony. 115 mules live on one of the Sanctuary's outlying farms, Town Barton, in Tedburn St Mary, near Exeter. Spread over a hundred and forty acres, it became a specialist farm for mules in 2005; it is also home to 158 donkeys.

The mules live in groups of between four and twenty. They are grouped according to individual needs, depending on what behavioural work is needed – a large number of them have a need for this. Of course, bonded friends always stay together, as it is the charity's policy that animals that have bonded with each other remain together for the rest of their lives.

Stable management for over a hundred mules is very different to managing one or two in a private home. The mules live in barns which are divided into sections with straw beds. Beds of wood shavings are used for mules with a tendency towards laminitis, as well as those on diets or with respiratory problems. This type of environment suits the mules as they can wander around, and interact with each other, therefore keeping themselves mentally stimulated. In the summer months each group is turned out in grass paddocks for several hours each day, and in the winter they have access to a 'sand school' to let off steam, as with such a large number of animals grass turnout in the winter months is impossible.

When Claire Shapcott came to work at The Donkey Sanctuary she had no idea what a mule was. In her words:

'As soon as I set eyes on one of these amazing animals I knew I wanted to learn more about them and work more closely with them. Luckily for me the management at the Sanctuary are very supportive and I was allowed to spend time working with mules with the help of Ben Hart, Manager of the Training Centre and a behavioural expert.

The first mule I worked with was called Wellington; he was a little boisterous and needed some extra handling. It wasn't as I expected, as I had no idea how intelligent mules were. I tried to train him like a horse and he outsmarted me many times! After spending a lot of time working with Wellington his behaviour improved and, accompanied by his donkey friend George he joined a family in a new home.

I met Wellington's new family at The Donkey Sanctuary's Mule Open Day, which was held at Town Barton Farm in September 2009. It was lovely to meet up with Wellington and George's new 'foster parents' and hear how well they are getting on in their new home!

I love working with mules because each one has its own character and a story to tell as to why they ended up in our care. No two are ever the same. It's hard not to become too attached to them and I always find it sad when much-loved friends pass on. There have been many favourites over the last nine years, including Henry, pictured here.'

Claire and Henry

DONKEYS

Naughty Face

In August 1969 I was glancing through the local newspaper when my eyes rested on a small advertisement: 'Pedigree donkey mare for sale, Kennetbury Martha – apply Mr Mogar'. The address wasn't too far from the Salston Hotel (which we had bought a few years previously), so the family piled into the car and went to see her. She exceeded all my dreams. She was a proper grey donkey colour with the most beautifully clear cross marked on her back. Her bones were fine and she had legs almost like a racehorse. Her head was beautiful, with the largest limpid brown eyes and the softest black muzzle. To add to my joy, it was explained that she was probably in foal! We fell in love at once and I couldn't wait to get her home. Mr Mogar promised to deliver her when we had fenced off a paddock and built a stable.

Kennetbury Martha's arrival was a much more significant event than I could possibly appreciate or foresee at the time. Down the ramp she trotted impertinently (did *she* know she was to be the first of over fourteen thousand?). I sat on the paddock rails watching her. Donkeys arriving in a new area are fairly predictable; they like to explore every corner and then return to indicate whether the new home is satisfactory or not! She returned to me, giving me such an enormous push with her head that I almost fell off the fence!

'Stop pushing me with that naughty face,' I mumbled, restoring my dignity as best I could. I then realised I had found a much better name for her than Kennetbury Martha – and Naughty Face she became.

Having approved her quarters she examined her stable minutely, checked that her water, hay and straw were up to standard, had a long roll and decided she was home. We talked together for a long time and during my evening's work in the hotel I kept making excuses to slip out and look at her.

Early morning is not the best time for hoteliers – we rarely got to bed before 2 am – but Naughty Face found the dawn lonely and her mournful brays brought less than appreciative comments from the rest of my family, to say nothing of the hotel guests! I decided that she needed a companion, so along came Angelina. Soon after Angelina's arrival Naughty Face gave birth to a dear little foal who I named 'Superdocious'.

As the years went by and the number of donkeys in my care increased, my love for Naughty Face never diminished, although it had to be shared with the other donkeys. When the donkeys and my family took up residence at Slade House Farm I was so proud of her on the many occasions when she called me out. She had a stable in the main yard not far from the bedroom windows and when there was a donkey in trouble it was always Naughty Face

Naughty Face was a very special donkey to me!

whose bray called me out. I'm sure she knew which bedroom I was in because as soon as the light went on she stopped braying. She knew I was on my way. One particular summer night when all the donkeys, except the very sick, were out at grass, there was a tremendous thunderstorm. In the middle of the storm came the unmistakable braying. Someone had to be in trouble. Niels and I dressed quickly. Naughty Face was calling from the valley that runs down to the sea and we found her in the light of a big torch braying mournfully by Beth, a recent arrival who, totally unexpectedly, had produced a foal! Thanks to Naughty Face's help both mother and foal were saved.

Naughty Face lived happily at The Donkey Sanctuary until the summer of 1992. I was devastated to lose her and I decided that she would be buried in what we call the Rose Garden at Slade House Farm. A plaque marks the spot where my very first donkey lies.

Norman

Norman

Norman came over to the UK from the Irish Sanctuary in a group of eight donkeys in June 2009. He is such a lovely friendly donkey and it was at first thought that he would benefit from working in the Education and Activities Department. Unfortunately he is very sensitive about having his teeth rasped and has to be sedated every time the Sanctuary's dental technician

comes on the scene. It was decided that Norman would benefit from living in New Barn, where he can mix with the visitors and wander around the main yard enjoying all the attention!

Swanthorpe Dusty aka Nutella!

Nutella

I have to admit that we do come across some difficult and naughty donkeys!

One example was a two-year-old black and white stallion whose official name was Swanthorpe Dusty, although he was known, for some reason, as Nutella! He had been living at a children's 'petting farm' since he was seven months old, but it was felt he would have to go because his behaviour had become more and more aggressive. A lot of children visited the farm (including many who have special needs) and it was too risky to keep him. He kept rearing up and biting and, even worse, he had killed a goat (although this may have been an accident, as they used to play well together). His desperate owners considered having Nutella put to sleep, but decided instead to phone The Donkey Sanctuary. Following six weeks in the New Arrivals Unit and the regulation 'little operation', Nutella has now been moved to Brookfield Farm. He's a bright, intelligent donkey and hopefully he will enjoy a long and happy life there.

Nutty

Seven-year-old Nutty came into our care in July 2009 as she had a problem with sarcoids (growths), which had to be operated on soon after she arrived.

Nutty

Her previous owners had bought Nutty because they felt sorry for her. They'd actually gone to view a donkey that she was with, and ended up bringing them both home! Nutty then went on to grow quite large – over 14hh – and she used her size to her advantage. She kept escaping from her field and chasing the owners' Shetland ponies around. It was decided that The Donkey Sanctuary was the best place for her, offering a more challenging environment. Nutty's owners still come and visit her at the Sanctuary.

DONKEY FACTS, PEOPLE AND PLACES

Nepal – our work there

The Donkey Sanctuary helps fund the Animal Nepal group which works with the donkeys in the brick kilns at Kathmandu. Donkey welfare in these Nepalese kilns is absolutely appalling. Animal Nepal has been operating mobile clinics in the kilns and educating owners and labourers since 2008, and has also been introducing an improved type of harness designed by the Donkey Sanctuary India. Animal Nepal is now extending its work to the off-season period, June to December. During this time the donkeys are taken from the kilns back to the Nepaljung area, the main entrance point for donkeys smuggled over the border from India and also the location of the main equine

Donkeys carrying bricks in Nepal

bazaar. Here they are left to scavenge for food in the streets, at risk of road accidents and attacks by shopkeepers.

Animal Nepal started a two-year programme in 2010 to improve the conditions of working equines during the off-season and also to stop the illegal import of unsuitable equines into Nepal. The Donkey Sanctuary is helping to finance this work. We are also hoping to strengthen the existing links with our project in India and offer help with the educational side of Animal Nepal's work.

Not Just Donkeys

Since my work with donkeys began I have written over forty books for both children and adults. Some of the children's books were published by Pan and Piccolo many years ago, and then one day in 1983, I met Annabel Whittet. She was an amazing woman, totally involved in publishing books on all species of wildlife. At that time I was thinking of writing a book on donkeys for two reasons: to make the public, particularly children, more aware of donkeys, and to raise desperately needed funds for the Sanctuary.

A drawing of the delightful church at Tedburn St Mary features on the book's front cover

Annabel became a friend of mine, and we worked together for over thirty years. The latest book she published for me was *Not Just Donkeys*, a simple book of interesting stories and poems. I have often written short poems over the years, which are read at our annual Memorial Day service as well as at the service held during Donkey Week at the beautiful church adjoining our farm at Tedburn St Mary. The Sanctuary's Chief Executive, David Cook, persuaded me to gather some of these poems together in a book as, according to him, many people wanted to read them.

The last time I met Annabel was in Swindon in June 2008, where we finalised the text and illustrations for the book. Less than five months later I received a telephone call to advise me that she had died. To say I was shocked was an understatement. She was far too young to die and I have missed her terribly.

I'm glad to say Annabel's publishing company, Whittet Books Limited, has continued and the book was published just a few months before she died. The poems in this book are dedicated to Annabel's memory.

DONKEYS

Oliver

Poor little Oliver! He was an eight year old stallion who had been tied up tightly and then abandoned by his owner in County Clare, Ireland. Our Welfare Officer, Lucy Hunt, was appalled when she saw the condition of his hooves, as they were grossly overgrown. Lucy rang the local Gardaí, who were extremely helpful, taking the responsibility of signing Oliver over to our Irish Sanctuary.

Oliver had to be transported very carefully, as obviously his balance was badly affected. As soon as he arrived his feet were treated by our farrier. He is such a gentle, sweet-natured donkey and all the staff are very fond of him. Following his time in our isolation unit, he joined a group of donkeys that have had similar problems. He will have a happy life from now on.

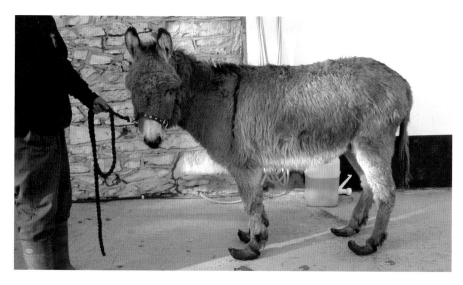

Oliver's feet were in a terrible state

Ollie

Ollie came into The Donkey Sanctuary in 2008 and initially he settled down at Woods Farm. However, it became evident that he would be ideal for one of the EST Centres, as he was so good-natured and was an ideal size. Since he's been at the Leeds Centre he has made friends with Mowbray and Eli and the three of them are always up to mischief. Ollie's favourite trick is to remove another donkey's coat, and the photograph shows him sharing the fun with Mowbray.

Ollie up to his tricks!

Oscar (1) at EST Birmingham

Oscar (1)

Oscar is one of our EST team of donkeys in Sutton Park, near Birmingham. He arrived at The Donkey Sanctuary in 1995 having previously lived in the New Forest area with two other donkeys, some goats and some horses. His owner relinquished him to the Sanctuary as she was suffering from arthritis and was no longer able to look after him.

When Oscar first arrived he was a very nervous young donkey but he has now grown in confidence and has become very cheeky and loves to play. Nothing can happen at the Centre without Oscar – at least that is how he sees it. If he isn't helping the children by either giving them rides or pulling their cart, he bangs on the arena door with his front hoof demanding to come in to watch. He often steals brooms and runs away, and he's even been known to take hold of another donkey's lead rope and pull him along – perhaps he wants to be a member of staff as well!

Oscar (2)

Meet Oscar, the baby of the Leeds EST Centre. At five years old he may be the Centre's youngest donkey but he is definitely showing that he is one of the cleverest. He has a siesta most afternoons and lies down on the yard, which can be a bit of a sun trap. The staff couldn't believe their eyes one day when they saw he had pulled his stable bedding outside into the sunshine and settled down on it for a snooze!

Oscar loves to share a cup of tea with the staff when they have their morning break.

Oscar (2), having his morning cuppa!

DONKEY FACTS, PEOPLE AND PLACES

Outreach programme

Many of the donkeys at the EST Centres play a major part in our Outreach programme, where they are taken to visit schools and special needs education centres, hospices and day care centres, as well as, hospitals and residential care homes.

The donkeys are chosen very carefully for their calm and patient temperament and impeccable behaviour. As well as these characteristics, they must really enjoy human interaction. To prepare them for Outreach work they undergo a high level of training, making full use of the facilities around the EST Centres to get them used to being indoors and going up and down steps and stairs.

The health and safety of both the donkeys and the people we visit are of paramount importance and the donkeys are never made to go anywhere or behave in any way they are not happy with.

The visits mean so much to the residents of the hospices, hospitals and care homes, and are a major talking point for them. In turn, it's a privilege to be welcomed by such a wonderful group of people who benefit so much from the stimulation their contact with our donkeys gives them.

On visits to Holmsley, a nursing home in Sidmouth, one of our donkeys, Mary, walks up the main entrance steps, in through the front door, across a carpeted hall and into the lounge, where she meets some of the residents, including Kay, who is 89 years old. Kay looks forward to seeing the donkeys when they visit, and says it's the highlight of her week. Mary is always beautifully behaved and never leaves any 'surprises' behind!

Vera, aged 84, is a resident at The Check House in Seaton, Devon, and she loves to see the donkeys when they visit. Vera suffers from arthritis and high blood pressure and says that the visits have such a calming effect on her.

LEFT *Kay enjoying a chat with Mary*

Vera loves the donkeys' visits

DONKEYS

Paddy

Paddy was in a terrible condition when he arrived at our Sanctuary in County Cork in Ireland in 2009. He had been rescued from a field in West Cork and he was suffering with appallingly overgrown feet as well as an untreated injury to his hind leg, caused by a piece of ingrown wire.

Donkeys should have their feet trimmed every six to eight weeks so it was evident that he had been neglected for a very long time. Paddy Barrett, Public Relations Manager for the charity, told me:

> 'We had our doubts as to whether or not Paddy would make it. His hooves were horribly long and painful, as they had not been trimmed for quite some time.
>
> Our caring staff were able to tend to his feet and his wound and we are pleased that he is making a good recovery. Paddy is making new friends in a special group for donkeys with foot problems and remains under the watchful eye of our experienced grooms and veterinary team.'

Paddy and Crumble

Some donkeys have come into the Sanctuary with unusual companions over the years! (*see note overleaf*) Sometimes donkeys become inseparable from their friends and, of course, we would never tear them apart. Companions have included chickens, ducks, goats, ponies and horses and, if we feel the bond is genuine, then we grant them the same privileges we give to all donkeys – love, care and attention for the rest of their natural lives.

ABOVE *Paddy enjoying Crumble's unique method of grooming!*

Paddy's feet were in an appalling condition

Paddy was over forty years of age and had lived with his friend for over twenty years. Crumble was an extremely large Jersey cross cow! We understood that if we didn't take Crumble she would be shot, so in she came. She was a really lovely, gentle animal, spending her days licking Paddy constantly with her long, rough tongue. They had to have special quarters allocated to them, as not all our donkey shelters could accommodate such a large friend!

Note For disease control reasons it is no longer possible to accommodate cloven hoofed animals at the Sanctuary.

Pansy

Pansy is a very clever donkey! She can open stable doors with her teeth, which is amazing, as she only has two at the front! When she finds that the donkeys on special feeds have been shut in while they eat, she clamps her teeth around the bolt and pulls it back, so that she can have her share! The staff have to watch her carefully and have put clips on the doors to make sure Pansy doesn't break in. Her two front teeth have prompted the staff to nickname her 'the stapler'! The photograph opposite shows her in action!

Peanuts

I never get over the miracle of birth – especially where donkeys are concerned. We knew we could have problems with the 'in foal' mares we had rescued

jointly with the RSPCA and we'd already had two foals born within the group during Easter 2000. We were all keeping a special eye on the remainder of the group, looking carefully for the first signs of foaling. However the first call came from Woods Farm, where another donkey was also in foal. After discovering that the mare was pregnant, it had been decided that she should have her foal at Woods Farm rather than give her the stress of moving her to the hospital.

Unfortunately when the foal was born in May, both her front legs were twisted, so with her mother, Nina, she had to be brought to Slade House Farm. The foal's main problem was exacerbated by the fact that her mother didn't accept her, which caused even more concern. However dedicated nursing ensured her survival; she was bottle-fed every two hours day and night, while Nina stood watching, apparently quite happy to let us do the work. Two of our vets, Alex and Vicky, made little splints for her front legs, and with daily changing of the splints it was soon clear that the treatment was working. After ten

Peanuts has grown into a strong, healthy donkey

days the splints were finally removed and she was able to stand unaided, and a few days later she was enjoying her first outing in one of the hospital paddocks.

Almost twenty-five years previously I had experienced an identical problem with a new born donkey when Niels and I were running the Salston Hotel. I'd named that little foal 'Peanuts', so we christened this new foal with the same name.

Having been bottle-reared from birth she enjoyed the companionship of both humans and donkeys and she and her friends Aurora, Grace, Bert, Bandy, Tamarón and Jessie (the foals born to the recently rescued donkeys), together with their mothers, were put together in a barn and paddock, which we call 'Clifford Smith', where they were a constant source of interest and amusement for our many visitors. As the foals grew it was decided that they deserved to be with people who could give them more individual care, so they were considered for placing in 'foster homes'. Peanuts, along with her friend, Aurora, went to live at Bridgend College in Wales, where students train in equine welfare. They soon settled in their new home, where they receive lots of 'hands-on' attention from the students and staff alike.

Ponk

Ponk was born into the safety of The Donkey Sanctuary in 2004 to Grumps (see story under 'Grumps, Donks and Jenny') and, as he grew, he became a good candidate for our Show Team, as he was a perfect donkey both in conformation and nature. The Show Team donkeys are taken to the many agricultural shows held in the South West, where they are entered into donkey classes and are available for 'hands-on' contact with the general public. He took to 'showing' like a duck to water, as he loves all the fuss and cuddles that he receives. In 2008 he won the 'best turned-out and condition' at Totnes Show.

We plan to teach Ponk to pull a cart soon, and we are also considering training him to pull a plough so that he could take part in ploughing matches. According to Maxine Carter, manager of Slade House Farm, he is her 'little star'!

Ponk has an additional claim to fame as mascot of The Donkey Sanctuary's children's club, Donkidz. He has a girlfriend named Pink (for obvious reasons, as she has pink hooves)! Within the confines of Donkidz Ponk is a lazy little blighter, who doesn't do a lot really – although the real Ponk is much more energetic! Donkidz issued a regular mazagine for its members until Spring 2010, but from Christmas 2010 issues are available on-line, free of charge.

Ponk as a foal, with his mother, Grumps

DONKEY FACTS, PEOPLE AND PLACES

Peru

We help fund the Asociacion Humanitaria San Francisco de Asis, an organisation based in Colan near the north-west coast of Peru, which works to improve animal welfare in the rural villages of that area through veterinary and community initiatives. There are high levels of poverty and a lack of education among animal owners, leading to neglect (some of it unintentional). The charity runs mobile clinics and an animal rehabilitation centre as well as an education programme in schools. The Donkey Sanctuary provides funding to help make affordable veterinary and farriery services available to donkeys and mules in the area, and educate children in primary schools on donkey care.

Rosemary Gordon, who runs the Asociacion, told us the story of the donkey in the photo (*see overleaf*).

'We came across this little donkey, whose name I do not know, when doing our clinics in a village called Pueblo Nuevo where we go every Friday to work. He had pulled the cart from his owner's smallholding with a flat tyre on the cart, and with the heavy load he was carrying on arrival simply collapsed. It was a sorry sight. We asked the owner what had happened and he simply said that the donkey was tired, so we immediately helped take the load off the cart and got the donkey to stand. We reprimanded the owner and told him that the load was far too heavy, and that the donkey needed to be taken care of in order that it could work for him for many more years.'

Rosemary has not been able to keep track of that particular donkey or owner, but says:

'Together with The Donkey Sanctuary we have been able to assist many donkeys and have definitely reached many children with the message that donkeys matter and they should have more care and attention.'

The owner said the donkey was 'tired'!

Violet Philpin

Although donkeys had always been my favourite animals it wasn't until I became aware of the work of Violet Philpin that I realised what a huge need there was to help these humble, gentle animals.

In the 1950s Miss Philpin began to take abandoned animals into her care, and she set up a charity known as the Helping Hand Animal Welfare League Donkey Sanctuary which she ran in Woodley, near Reading in Berkshire. She was a familiar sight in the area, driving around in her little old car; rumour has it that, because her car had no heating system she often had a paraffin heater burning in the passenger foot well to keep her warm! She was certainly eccentric – but she had a heart of gold!

As Miss Philpin became elderly the work became almost impossible for her and she had to resort to placing large groups of donkeys into care of other people, paying them two pounds per donkey per week. Her land and buildings began to deteriorate badly and her failing health prevented her from being able to cope. On several occasions she had phoned me asking if I would take into care donkeys in a very bad condition that she couldn't cope with.

I continued to assist, until one day in 1973 I received a telephone call from a Mr Holman of Barclays Bank to say that Miss Philpin had died and I had been named as a residuary legatee in her Will. I was shocked to say the least, as I knew straight away that this wasn't going to be a simple matter of a cheque arriving in the post. I was right – I had inherited 204 donkeys!

Immediate panic set in, especially when I learned that there was insufficient feed available for the donkeys and no money to buy more. In fact the charity was some £8,400 in debt. After attending the funeral the executor and I went to Miss Philpin's Sanctuary together and I was horrified to see that there weren't in fact 204 donkeys – rather more like eighty or ninety. The remainder had been boarded out in various parts of the country.

Luckily the sale of Miss Philpin's house covered a lot of the bills, and I received enormous help from the Charity Commissioners, who advised me on the best way to handle the situation. It was agreed that my charity (at that time the South Western Donkey Sanctuary), should be amalgamated with the Helping Hand Animal Welfare League and, with the loan of a large barn at Farway

Miss Philpin with some of her donkeys, watched by young admirers
Reproduced with the kind permission of George Konig, Keystone Press Agency Getty Images

Countryside Park, the donkeys would be brought down to Devon. It took several months to collect all the donkeys that had been boarded out, but in they all came to what was now known as The Donkey Sanctuary. The need for a farm to house them on a permanent basis became a priority and I was fortunate enough to find Slade House Farm near Sidmouth, which remains the charity's headquarters to this day.

Ploughing donkeys

Contributed by Ann Veit, Secretary, Colaton Raleigh and District Ploughing Association

I think most people are aware that in many parts of the world donkeys still work pulling ploughs. I first became aware of The Donkey Sanctuary at Sidmouth through my role as secretary of the Colaton Raleigh and District Ploughing Association and Dr Svendsen's interest in putting donkeys to the plough at the Association's annual ploughing match.

When I was first asked to become secretary of the Association my knowledge of ploughing was very basic and, in truth, the technicalities are still a bit of a mystery. I was assured by the retiring secretary that the ploughs were not raced up and down a field, and that the quality of the ploughing was the important factor. Judges spend the day checking starting furrows, uniformity of work, finishing of furrows and many other characteristics known only to the competition ploughman.

The venue for the ploughing match rotates up and down the East Devon coast between Sidmouth and Exeter, stopping off at Colaton Raleigh on the way. This means that once every three years we actually have the ploughing match on Sanctuary land. Each year a President is elected from among our

Taking my turn at the plough

many Vice Presidents to preside at the match and present the trophies. At Sidmouth our President is invariably Dr Svendsen.

Dr S, as President, arrives promptly to judge the flowers, crafts and children's entries before presiding over the judges' lunches and catching up with members of the Association, most of whom she has known for many years. This is a jolly time – made jollier by Dr S's presence.

Almost every year Dr S. does a ploughing demonstration with a specially made plough to show how these beautiful beasts can also be very useful. I remember one year the grooms were leading a couple of beautiful chocolate coloured donkeys in harness to the plough while Dr S. steered the plough. They came to the end of the prepared plot but were enjoying themselves so much they tried to carry on into the unprepared ground. They were eventually successfully turned and ploughed in the reverse direction. They certainly enjoyed the attention they got and I feel would have happily gone on for hours.

Poitou donkeys

The Poitou breed was developed in France for the sole purpose of producing large, strong working mules. There was a huge demand for working donkeys until the 1940s and at the height of their popularity the Poitou region of France produced up to thirty thousand a year. However, as draught animals were replaced with motor vehicles there was less reason to breed them and their numbers quickly declined.

The Poitou donkey is easily recognisable for a number of unusual characteristics that distinguish it from other donkeys. It is much larger, standing between 1.35m and 1.50m (14.1/14.3hh), has a large head and enormous ears. Its long, shaggy coat is always brown or black, often with a white underbelly. Despite their size, Poitou donkeys are gentle and friendly.

In the 1980s I became aware of the fact that the Poitou donkey was becoming an endangered species and that there were probably less than two hundred pure-bred Poitous in existence. Bob Camac, one of the Trustees of The International Donkey Protection Trust (since amalgamated with The Donkey Sanctuary) had visited France to see how the Sanctuary could help, and we had been working in fairly close co-operation, receiving a visit from one of the world experts on the Poitou, Jacques Moreau, to discuss the way forward to preserve the breed. In 1988 we sent our senior vet, John Fowler, over to France to have a look at the situation and to offer help with donkey welfare and management. June Evers and I were invited to visit SABAUD (Association de Sauvegarde du Baudet du Poitou), an association set up to save the Poitou, and they took the unusual step of allowing two of their mares out of the country to be cared for by The Donkey Sanctuary. Jonquille was thirteen years old and the other donkey was a very elderly mare by French standards. Her name was

A group of Poitou donkeys at the Sanctuary

Amande who, at twenty-two years old was past breeding. She came along purely as a companion to Jonquille. They promised that they would let us have a suitable stallion who was not related to Jonquille in the hope that we would be able to breed successfully in the UK should the project in France fail. They kept their promise and Torrent arrived later in the year.

Although the Sanctuary has a 'no-breeding' policy, it was felt that an exception to the rule on a minor scale would help to protect the future of this magnificent animal. The breeding programme was only for short time and the Sanctuary currently has six pure-bred Poitou donkeys.

Portugal – our work there

- Our licensed holding base in Portugal is in the village of Miranda do Duoro in the north of Portugal, close to its border with Spain. There are many working donkeys in this region.
- Miguel, the owner of the holding base, is a vet, and every year we fund him to provide welfare treatments to donkeys in the surrounding area, as well as caring for the donkeys in his charge.

- By helping the locals to look after their own donkeys the welfare standards have improved generally, and the improvements in their care have resulted in only donkeys with major problems having to be brought into the holding base.
- The holding base can accommodate up to thirty donkeys and twenty-five are currently in care.

Donkeys help with the olive harvest in Portugal

DONKEYS

Quasar

In May 2010 a new foal was born to Silvia (see her story under 'S') at Il Rifugio del Asinelli. He was named as a result of a competition on the Italian Sanctuary's web site. A hundred and fifty suggestions were received and a little girl attending a grooming day at the Sanctuary, drew the winning name.

The meaning of 'Quasar' is 'the most luminous object in the universe', and we wish the new foal a bright future – just like his name. He is the 114th donkey to come under IRDA's care.

Queenie

The Clews family has worked with donkeys on Blackpool beach for many years, and Queenie was with them for seventeen years, giving rides to children. However, she developed arthritis in her back legs and, as with fifty-eight of the Clews' donkeys over the years, she was retired to The Donkey Sanctuary in 1999.

Queenie now lives on one of our outlying farms, East Axnoller, near Beaminster in Dorset, and is enjoying a quiet and peaceful life for the rest of her days.

Quincy and Xerxes

In June 2010 we were shocked to be advised of two donkeys in North Wales that had suffered seriously damaged hooves during their owner's botched attempt to trim their feet using a carpenter's chisel.

Quasar is featured on Il Rifugio's 2011 calendar

Queenie, with her friends, Tommy and Cheeky – all retired to the Sanctuary by the Clews family

Quincy meets a new friend!

The RSPCA had approached the owner of the two stallions several months previously, as their inspector was concerned that the donkeys were underweight and had long feet. The owner was advised that the donkeys desperately needed farriery treatment, but no arrangements were made and he was advised to sign the donkeys over to us for the sake of their health. However, shortly before they were due to be collected, the owner decided that he would trim their feet himself using a chisel. This reckless and brutal act left both animals struggling with dreadfully painful damaged feet.

Both donkeys, now named Quincy and Xerxes, were taken to our Derbyshire Centre, near Buxton, where they are receiving intensive farriery treatment to rectify the damage. Under careful dietary control their weight is now increasing to a more healthy level. They will remain there until they are fit enough to be brought down to Devon.

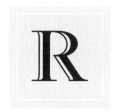

DONKEYS

Rainbow

In 1999 we started a new project at The Donkey Sanctuary called 'Donkey Facilitated Therapy', which involved visiting residential homes for the elderly in the East Devon area. Rainbow had been with us for over fifteen years and spent his time giving rides to children with special educational needs and disabilities. However, he was retired having developed a foot problem. It soon became obvious that he was missing working with the children as, when donkeys were selected for each day's riding, Rainbow was always waiting at the field gate hoping to be chosen. So we decided to see if he would like to become part of this new project.

What a success it was! He really enjoyed going into the residents' rooms and brought such excitement and pleasure to many elderly people. In one case, a very elderly lady, who spent her days in her own little world, never leaving her comfortable seat nor taking part in any activities, suddenly became inspired by Rainbow's visit. She got up, took hold of the lead rein and walked off with him, very closely monitored by staff and carers, who had never seen her so animated! Many comments received have included 'I've been looking forward to the donkeys coming all week', 'I will dream of the donkeys tonight' and 'they are a joy to have here' has proved the worth of the project.

Richie

Richie is a lovely young donkey now based at our Knockardbane Farm in Ireland. He was born on 15th January 2007 but sadly he was orphaned ten days later when his mother died from blood poisoning. Richie's owners were

Rainbow found new friends in residential homes

desperate for our help. Staff made an urgent journey in the snow to rescue him and bring him back to the Irish Sanctuary where he required round-the-clock care. He was bottle-fed milk substitute for several weeks, but he quickly took to feeding from a bucket on his own.

Despite his rough start in life, Richie has grown into a handsome, boisterous but well-liked young fellow. He is known for his hearty appetite and playful antics, and is a real winner with the visitors, especially children, who can't resist his charm and good looks.

Richie is definitely an outgoing, up-close kind of donkey – usually first up to the fence to check out any visitors, and he loves to run around and play as

BELOW LEFT *Richie being brought into care when only ten days old*

BELOW RIGHT *He has grown into a fine-looking donkey!*

roughly as possible. He will be your best friend so long as you play by his rules! He's an early riser as well, particularly during the summer months. Often when the farm staff arrive for work in the morning he will be holding the 'treat bucket' in his mouth and banging it on the gate! He just can't wait for his breakfast!

Romero

Romero is a very special donkey at El Refugio del Burrito, as he was the first to be taken into care in Spain. He came from the well-known town of Mijas, where donkey taxis are the main attraction for the thousands of visitors to this mountainside village. He spent most of his life carrying tourists in the village, but he became lame in one of his front legs and his owner decided to retire him to the Sanctuary.

Although he's worked very hard for many years, twenty-eight-year-old Romero is a still a very active donkey and, despite having a strong character, he is now behaving very well. He considers himself to be the 'king of the castle' at the farm and enjoys his contact with visitors under his new role of an adoption donkey – a just reward for all those years of hard work.

Romero enjoying life at El Refugio

Rosie

Rosie is a broken-coloured mare, born in 1989, who was taken into The Donkey Sanctuary's care in 1990. One of our Welfare Officers was contacted by the RSPCA who had been informed about a farmer whose animals were in a terrible condition. Rosie and two other donkeys were rescued, along with many more animals. The farmer was later fined and banned from keeping animals for ten years.

Living on one of the Sanctuary's outlying farms, it soon became obvious to staff that Rosie would be ideal to work with disadvantaged children, as she is very gentle. She came through her training with flying colours, the only problem being that Annie, one of her trainers, fell in love with her and wanted to keep her! In Rosie's best interests, though, she was transferred to work at the EST Leeds Centre, where she loves her work with the children.

Recently Rosie has been a very busy donkey, working on our Outreach project. As the visits to schools and hospices increase, she is becoming very well-travelled, thoroughly enjoying her trips in the lorry. She has lots of patience and loves being cuddled by everyone, children and adults alike – we think she enjoys being the centre of attention and stealing the limelight!

Rosie – a very busy donkey!

Ruby, Simba and Arthur

Ruby and Simba are mother and son. They were found, along with Simba's father, Arthur, on a caravan site in Wales. The adult donkeys' feet were very long and twisted and they were in a bad condition. Their owner was a man who travelled a great deal and neglected the donkeys in his absence. The RSPCA took the donkeys into their care at Gonsal Farm, near Shrewsbury, in April 2007, when Simba was only three months old.

Following the successful prosecution of the owner, the donkeys were relinquished to The Donkey Sanctuary in January 2008.

Ruby with foal, Simba

Rupert, Cocoa and Misty

On 24 August 2009 we received an email from a lady who told us the story of how she had lost track of her donkeys around ten years ago. I'm sure you will be interested to read her story:

'In approximately 1971 we went to view a male donkey for sale. He was called Rupert, and was around two years old. We simply could not leave his 'girlfriend' behind, so we bought Cocoa as well! Unbeknown to us they were expecting a foal and some months later they produced Misty for us. Unfortunately a few years later we lost our rented grazing, and we could not afford to put all three donkeys in livery. My brother's schoolteacher offered to take them as 'lawnmowers' for his four acres of land, and we agreed, as long as he promised to keep them as a family. For many years we saw them living a wonderful life, until about ten years ago, when we heard that the schoolteacher had passed away. We never found out what had happened to the donkeys, so I was obviously delighted when I heard from a friend of mine, who had spent a holiday in Sidmouth, that he had visited the Sanctuary and had found Rupert and Misty! Although he was told that Cocoa had sadly passed away, he could see that Rupert and his daughter Misty were enjoying a wonderful life with you.

I would dearly love to see them, and hope to arrange a visit as soon as possible. It was such a thrill for us to know that the promise of them 'always being a family' has come true and they spent their entire lives together. Thank you so very much.'

Rupert and Misty with Carole from our Welfare Department

Russell

Russell, Angelina's son was a very handsome donkey as well as having a lovely nature. He was so calm and friendly that when he was old enough he became one of the first donkeys to work with children with special educational needs and disabilities at The Slade Centre (now EST Sidmouth), where he worked happily for many years. In 1999 he was retired from his duties, but as he was still fit, active and very well-behaved he joined the Education and Activities team, which takes donkeys to visit children in mainstream schools as well as attending various fundraising exercises. He died in 2006 at thirty-one years old, but he has left a lasting legacy. As he was so perfect in size and conformation the life-sized bronze donkeys in our Memorial Garden at The Donkey Sanctuary and at our EST Centres in Birmingham, Manchester, Leeds and Ivybridge are modelled on him.

Russell – a perfect model for a donkey statue!

DONKEY FACTS, PEOPLE AND PLACES

Romania – our work there

- There are terrible problems in Romania for donkeys due to the poverty in the country and the fact that there is a thriving donkey meat trade.
- Our licensed holding base, which is run through the charity, 'Save the Dogs and other Animals', opened in 2007, and is situated in Cernavoda, 130 km east of Bucharest. A recent increase in size now enables it to care for up to eighty donkeys.
- Eight-nine donkeys have been taken into care so far; thirty-two of them have since been transferred to Il Refugio di Asinelli in Italy.

- The donkeys being saved are mainly from Dobrogea, a province in the south-east of the country, but we also have donkeys from Bucharest, Calarasi, Oltenite and Guigui.
- The star of the holding base is Rigoletto, who came from the national circus. In 2009 he won a contest by being voted for to become the boyfriend of Fiona, a star female donkey from a national television station. Of the 34,000 people who voted, he won over fifty per cent of the votes!

Donkeys at our holding base in Romania

Rigoletto, a Romanian celebrity!

S

DONKEYS

Shocks

In January 2010 the Irish Sanctuary received a call from a concerned member of the public who had seen a young donkey that was clearly in a great deal of distress and pain.

The donkey, called Shocks, had been kept with a rope tied so tightly around his neck that it had become deeply and painfully embedded. The owner had removed the rope by force, without giving Shocks any anaesthetic, and then attempted to clean the wound by pouring a bottle of abrasive chemical cleaning fluid over the donkey's neck, causing serious skin burns.

Bernard O'Neill, Welfare Manager at the Liscarroll Sanctuary told me, 'We found this donkey in a terrible state; his experience must have been excruciatingly painful for him. We were worried whether or not he would survive the trauma of his injuries but, with specialist veterinary attention and tender loving care from our staff, he has responded to his treatment well.'

In July 2010 Shocks was brought over to the UK and is now enjoying meeting new friends here.

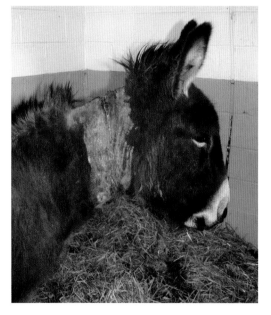

Shocks had suffered a terrible ordeal

Sierou

Cyprus was experiencing a mild start to the winter of 2009, but it was a dull, overcast day when Donkey Sanctuary (Cyprus) received a telephone call from an elderly farmer who lived in the village of Malia, Limassol District. He had a female donkey which he no longer required for work and was unable to feed through the winter, so he felt his only solution was to shoot her. He had been talking about his problem in the local coffee shop in the hope that a villager might take the donkey, and fortunately he was overheard by the Mukhtar (the Mayor), who told the farmer about The Sanctuary at Vouni. The following day the farmer telephoned the Sanctuary and asked if we would take his donkey. Of course, Farm Manager, Richard Davies, agreed, and arrangements were made to pick her up. Welfare Officer, Gill Powell tells the story:

Sierou

'It had to happen – early morning saw the first of the winter's heavy rains, so with my driver, Petros, I set out for Malia village, about half an hour's journey from Vouni. The roads were extremely slippery and we had trouble keeping the horsebox on the twisting mountain road. We arrived at Malia village square where we were to meet the owner with the donkey. We waited and waited but there was no sign of either. The wind was blowing and the rain was lashing down; we were very cold and wet. While we were making a telephone call to the office for instructions a man arrived and told us the farmer no longer had the donkey. Fearing the worst – that the farmer had shot her – we started to leave the square, and then suddenly in the distance we saw a man with a very wet, bedraggled donkey walking towards us. Was it our donkey? Yes, it was Sierou.

We stopped and opened the door of the horsebox, and the poor donkey walked slowly up the ramp. She was very cold and wet so I gave her a quick examination to make sure she was fit to travel, then we rubbed her down with straw to warm her. The owner signed our paperwork and said how grateful he was that we could take her.

We set off on our journey home; the weather became worse as mist and low cloud came down. It was very slow going; Sierou was nervous and restless in the box so we had to make several stops to ensure she was all right. The half hour journey took one hour and fifteen minutes but we arrived back at the Sanctuary safe and sound.

During our absence the grooms had made ready a loosebox in the isolation wing, bedding it up with fresh straw. Sierou was taken into the box and I'm sure you could see the delight on her face at being warm and dry at last. She was found to have a skin condition and a lot of her hair was missing on her flanks and shoulder, but after treatments with medicated shampoo and regular grooming, her hair has now grown back nicely. While she was receiving the treatment she required a donkey rug to keep her warm on cold nights.

Sierou is a very gentle, affectionate donkey and loves to play and have cuddles from the staff. She has settled well in what is called "pensioner's field", where she was felt to be the most comfortable, as she's a very shy girl and interacts better with the older, quieter donkeys.'

Silvia and Poldo

Following a report from a concerned member of the public, the Italian authorities went to investigate the condition of two donkeys in the Biella area of northern Italy who were suffering from shocking levels of starvation and neglect. The authorities acted quickly and decisively to confiscate the donkeys from their owner and they contacted our Italian Sanctuary, Il Rifugio Degli Asinelli (IRDA).

Silvia and Poldo were taken into care on 29 January 2010. They were found to be in a very poor condition, extremely thin, covered with lice and with hooves that were painfully long. Silvia, in particular, had problems walking. Paul Svendsen, our Director of European Operations, told me: 'We were shocked when we first saw the condition of Silvia and Poldo. There is little doubt that, without the fast action of the local authorities and the hard work of our staff, these animals would not have made it. They both have such lovely natures and it's been wonderful to see them returning to the healthy, happy donkeys they deserve to be.'

Over the next few months the donkeys' weights increased regularly and their feet improved. Sylvia became able to walk properly. However, there was a surprise in store!

In May Barbara Massa (IRDA's General Manager) reported: 'IRDA is happy to announce a new birth! On 11 May, Silvia gave birth to a beautiful male foal. He is in a perfect condition, vital and curious as only foals can be. Silvia is a protective mother, but after few days she permitted us to approach her baby. He's absolutely beautiful!'

IRDA organised a competition via the Italian Sanctuary's website to find a name for its latest arrival – the 114th donkey to come under its care. The name chosen was Quasar and there is a lovely photograph of him under 'Q'.

Silvia with her foal, Quasar

Simon

Simon came from a loving home but in 1995 his owner was going away to college, so she reluctantly sent him into The Donkey Sanctuary's care.

The staff of the EST Centre near Leeds were delighted when their local television station 'Calendar' asked if they could spend a day travelling around with them on their Outreach work to film them as they took a donkey to local care homes. Simon was chosen to be the film star!

The day started early when Simon and his team set off to West Riding House Care Home at Wakefield. On arrival Simon was gently led into the main lounge area where he was greeted delightedly and patted by all the residents. He helped many of them take a fond trip down memory lane as they recalled and chatted about happy times of their association with donkeys in the past. Many of them remembered riding donkeys on the beach when they were younger.

Simon doesn't mind Sylvester the cat having a nap on his back!

After a few hours at the care home it was time for Simon to bid farewell and set off to his next booking, which was to help Father Christmas deliver gifts at the Riding for the Disabled children's Christmas party. Simon was a huge hit with the children, who all gave him plenty of hugs and kisses and a big bag of carrots for him and all the other donkeys to share over the holiday period.

The Calendar film crew produced a birds-eye view of EST's Outreach work, punctuated with Simon's occasional bray! This was shown on the ITV television station and he was invited along to the television studios for a live interview on the day. Needless to say he was a real star and even made his grand entrance into the studio on a red carpet!

Simon is also one of the Centre's adoption donkeys, so he is very used to the limelight. His previous owner continues to visit him regularly.

Smartie

Smartie's arrival in April 1973 was a dreadful shock. She had been delivered to me as an apparently normal donkey in perfect health. At the time of her arrival The Donkey Sanctuary had not yet been formed, but I was the South-West Area Representative for the Donkey Breed Society and a member had asked if I would help to acquire a donkey suitable for a family. As no members had a suitable animal, I saw one advertised in the local paper and arranged for her to be delivered to me so that I could make sure she would be a sound purchase. I wasn't there when she was delivered but when I arrived I was disturbed to find I couldn't get near her; she was obviously terrified and looked thin and

Smartie with her foal, Eeyore

scruffy. I thought it best to leave her with some feed and water nearby until she had settled.

My husband, Niels, and I were woken as dawn was breaking by the loud braying of the other donkeys. We dressed quickly and went to see what all the fuss was about and, to our horror we could see the new donkey collapsed in the grass, barely breathing. We decided to move her into a small shed near the back door and, to our surprise, we found that the two of us were able to lift her easily. Poor Smartie was too ill to be frightened now and lay, eyes shut, while we rugged her up and fixed an infrared lamp over her for warmth. While Niels rang the vet I spooned glucose and warm milk down her throat. All that long day we continued the treatment. On examination, the vet said she had been starved almost to death, and the prognosis was not good. However, he began a course of vitamin injections which, together the warmth and nourishment, brought her back to taking an interest in her surroundings.

By evening, after managing a little bran mash she stood up, and it was a unique moment for us both. I was able to start cleaning her up gently; handfuls of lice-infested hair came off in my hands as I brushed her. While I was doing this my young son, Clive, came in. Looking at the donkey, he said, 'she looks quite smart now' – so we decided to call her 'Smartie'.

I never paid a penny for her. I had a most traumatic meeting with the dealer who had advertised her. I invited him to the house and showed Smartie to him. He was a great actor and seemed genuinely surprised. 'I can't understand it,' he said, scratching his head. 'I got her in the market and she seemed the best of the bunch.' I shuddered to think what the rest had looked like. I told him I was going to bring a prosecution, but realised I was on shaky ground, as he had apparently bought her only a few days before he had delivered her to me – but the threat was enough. 'That's not the donkey I delivered here,' he said firmly. 'I don't want any money for her – you can keep her – never seen her before'! He slammed the door on the way out and drove off at full speed.

I was delighted by the way Smartie's character changed. She soon welcomed me with a bray every time I came into her stable and she was very gentle. She amazed the vet by her recovery; she began to put on weight and to lose her skeleton-like appearance. In fact, she began to put on rather too much weight and I began to feel a little suspicious. One night, as I sat with her I noticed a definite movement in the now bulging stomach. I laid my hand on her side and nearly had it pushed off by a hard kick by a little hoof somewhere in there!

I didn't want to leave her stable as her time drew near. She had been with me almost a year. Gestation for a donkey is between eleven and thirteen months, so I knew she must be nearly due. Most donkeys prefer to have their foals alone and can in fact stop the first stages of labour for quite a long period of time if they are disturbed. However, it is only too easy to lose the foal if the mare is weak, as the membrane bag in which it is born can be very tough and the foal can suffocate if the bag doesn't break naturally or if the mother doesn't bite it open. For this reason I kept a close eye on Smartie but I need not have bothered to set the alarm for hourly visits – an enormous bray jerked me into consciousness at 2.30am on 20th June 1974 and rushing to Smartie's stable, I found her in the last stages of labour, panting heavily. 'It's all right, Smartie,' I said, and she calmed down immediately. Seconds later out slithered the foal. He didn't need any help. With a few hefty movements he emerged from the bag, shook his head and reached out towards Smartie, who had turned to look in proud amazement. 'You've done it Smartie,' I cried in joy. 'It's a super little colt. What shall we call him?' To my surprise Smartie did the job – throwing her head up she gave a triumphant bray, 'Eeyore, Eeyore'! So we named the little foal who was to become the naughtiest donkey in the Sanctuary!

The story had a very sad ending. On 20th March 1981 Smartie was found dead in her stable. She'd had almost eight years of happiness in her life and the post mortem was inconclusive. One can only assume that eventually her brush with death due to starvation had shortened her expected life span. Fortunately Eeyore had already made firm friends with other donkeys and he was old enough and strong enough not to be affected too much.

Snowy in her face mask

Snowy

Snowy was born at Axnoller Farm in December 1995 to Mary, who had been relinquished to The Irish Donkey Sanctuary earlier that year. As Snowy grew up she made friends with a donkey named Vicky Eire. Both of them were chosen to join the donkey team at the EST Ivybridge Centre.

Summer sunshine can cause quite a problem for Snowy. She is a white donkey and has pink skin on her nose, ears, on her back and under her belly. It is necessary for her to have a high factor sun block applied to the areas which are at risk of getting burned and she also wears a face mask made of a mesh material that has a detachable nose flap and covers for her ears. The mesh is fine enough to enable Snowy to see through it, but prevents the harsh rays of the sun from burning her, as well as acting as a fly screen. She is therefore able to bask in the sun without suffering any harm.

As well as giving rides to the children in the arena Snowy has now learned to pull the cart and she also visits residential homes on the Outreach programme. She is proud to be part of EST Ivybridge's Adoption Scheme.

DONKEY FACTS, PEOPLE AND PLACES

The Slade Centre

The Slade Centre was the forerunner of what is now The Elisabeth Svendsen Trust for Children and Donkeys (EST). My love of children as well as donkeys had given me the idea of using donkeys to give riding therapy to disadvantaged children and in 1975 I set up a new charity to achieve this aim. At first a team of donkeys was, during the summer months, taken out to schools for children with special needs and disabilities. However, in 1978, and following a long struggle with the planning authorities, a custom-built Centre was erected within the grounds of The Donkey Sanctuary. My sister, Pat, was appointed as its first Principal and what follows is an account of her recollections.

This place is ace!

Contributed by Pat Feather, first Principal of The Slade Centre (now EST Sidmouth)

My sister, Elisabeth Svendsen, had worked tirelessly to persuade the local authority to grant planning permission to build a Riding Centre for children with special needs and disabilities at The Donkey Sanctuary – and she won eventually! I was given the honour of becoming the first Principal of the Centre (now called the EST Sidmouth Centre) – one which I found deeply rewarding.

It had never been done before; it was a new experience for me, for the children, the donkeys and the staff. A superb building with a riding arena, stalls for donkeys, a well-equipped play area and special toilet facilities was opened by the Marquis of Bath in December 1978.

For several years gentle donkeys had been taken to school playgrounds to give rides to the children, who looked forward to the therapy and fun on a weekly basis. This was cancelled all too often because of bad weather. Now our ambulance, with a lift for wheelchairs, brought children in from the area around Sidmouth.

The first day was unforgettable – a mixture of physically and mentally disadvantaged children came into the play area in what can only be called 'an exuberant manner', released from the confines of small classrooms. The space was quite overwhelmed by those who could move – and they did! It was, quite honestly, a riot – and we quelled it by opening the sliding doors to the soft, sanded riding arena and allowing them to let off steam!

The riding therapy was a tremendous success and we watched such beneficial progress, both physical and mental over the years. Its success has since been mirrored in other Centres, with the same format, in various parts of the UK.

One of the first impressions I formed of this unique experience, was the happy atmosphere generated by the children. Here was a day (or a half day) with no pressures; just a lovely ride on a soft, friendly donkey, lovely toys to play with, a hot, tasty lunch and staff who soon became used to the various special needs of the children. We had our rewards – some of them quite emotional – the autistic child who had never been known to speak saying 'donkey' as he rode around the arena and causing his teacher to dab her eyes; the totally blind boy who held my hand as I guided him into the Centre, asking, 'What is a donkey, Pat?' I could imagine his nervousness and took him to a donkey and let him run his hand from head to tail, explaining the physique, the saddle and the head collar – and I wish you could have seen the broad smile on his face as he sat on the saddle and felt the movement.

I think we all felt deep emotions, not only in those first days, but in every session. To have a wheelchair-bound little girl go past on her favourite donkey, saying, 'I'm like you now, aren't I, Pat?' as she smiled – on eye-level for once. Or the tiny cerebral palsied boy with his deformed legs in a 'scissor constriction', who in the second ride of the day was able to actually sit astride his donkey.

A Saturday Club was started so that parents could come and talk, have a coffee and watch their children ride. Their siblings came too, I

Pat with two of her donkey team outside The Slade Centre

think they needed a time to play. They can be given a tough life as parents need to concentrate on the brother or sister.

As the first Principal, an ex-primary school teacher, I had a lot to learn, as did the riding instructors and grooms. The daily routine was not always easy but it was always rewarding, and could not have been accomplished so proficiently without the reliable team of voluntary helpers, who assisted with leading the donkeys and supporting the children as they rode around the arena.

As for those donkeys – they were so patient, so gentle and so determined to be present at every session! The ones not 'on duty' brayed disconsolately when not selected for the day's work. They really seemed to know that these children needed special care. One dear little boy who could hardly walk, desperately wanted to lead a donkey round the arena – we supported him as he held the leading rein of his favourite donkey, Russell, and managed to take four or five steps. Russell looked down at this little leader and placed his hooves so as to avoid the child; he knew exactly what to do – and how happy he made a boy who, sadly, died a few months later.

As one small boy once said to me, 'This place is ace, Pat'.

South Africa – our work there

South Africa has some of the worst cart and harness problems we've seen anywhere. For the last few years we've been funding several small organisations which are working to improve donkey welfare in their areas.

For example, we have given annual grants to the De Rust Donkey Awareness Project since 2006. This organisation has been developing a donkey cart owner association, which allows users access to a workshop where carts and harness are repaired. The project also designed a four-wheeled cart with three shafts – this allows drivers to use a simple traditional harness instead of the more complicated and expensive type necessary for harnessing donkeys to a single-shaft cart primarily intended for oxen. The De Rust group has also trained donkey cart drivers, and generally been active in promoting donkey welfare.

We also support the Eseltjiesrus Donkey Sanctuary in McGregor. This organisation is providing refuge and care for abused, neglected and elderly donkeys, but is also very keen to promote a 'culture of caring' among both children and adults. Groups are invited to visit its sanctuary and interact with the donkeys; people with special needs particularly benefit from this. The organisation is also running a schools and community education programme and we support this by helping to pay for the development of educational material.

Meanwhile at the University of Pretoria's Faculty of Veterinary Science at Onderstepoort, we have run annual workshops for the last few years on aspects of donkey health and welfare, including hoof care and dentistry.

Donkeys at the Eseltjiesrus Donkey Sanctuary in McGregor

Spain – our work there

- The Donkey Sanctuary has been involved with donkey-related welfare issues in Spain since 1986.
- The first European Rescue Centre, El Refugio del Burrito (ERB), was set up in Spain in 2003. It is based at Fuente de Piedra, a forty-five minute drive north of Malaga. It currently provides care for over ninety resident donkeys.
- A second farm, Dona Rosa, in Bodonal de la Sierra near Badajoz, was purchased in 2007. This farm, comprising over thirty hectares, can house over 250 donkeys; at present there are over a hundred resident donkeys.
- Other European operational holding bases are administered from El Refugio. These are located in Romania, Greece, France and Portugal. Many rescued donkeys are rested in the holding bases before undertaking the long journey to southern Spain.
- ERB investigate cases of neglect, abuse, ill-treatment or abandonment, or any other welfare issues concerning donkeys or mules. It gets actively involved in causes that promote the enforcement of existing animal welfare laws, and aims to secure the best conditions for those animals that are still used for work.
- Various donkey exploitation events, such as taxi rides, fiestas and donkey racing are monitored in Spain, as are equine markets.
- To date, more than 500 donkeys and mules around Europe have been provided with refuge or helped in other ways by El Refugio del Burrito.
- Although Dona Rosa is not open to the public, the farm at Fuente de Piedra is open every day of the year and entry is free of change.

Donkeys at Dona Rosa, El Refugio's second farm

Donkey plight

Since 2007 El Refugio del Burrito has been fighting against the use of donkeys during the annual Feria de la Manzanilla at San Lúcar de Barrameda near Cadiz. The Feria (Festival) takes place during the first week in June. Donkeys were being rented out illegally by unscrupulous owners and ridden, often by more than one person at a time with the riders under the influence of alcohol. The donkeys were often beaten as they carried their drunken burdens throughout the night.

El Refugio and three other Spanish animal welfare associations have been battling against this illegal practice, and they united in a moral battle to denounce it at the Guardia Civil's headquarters. Representatives from El Refugio were present to highlight the plight of the donkeys and ask for a ban to be introduced. Evidence in the form of photographs and films was presented. The meeting with the authorities resulted in the ban of donkeys on the beach and, in June 2010, the festival went ahead without the use of donkeys.

El Refugio's General Manager, who played a key role in this campaign, told me, 'We are so pleased we have been successful in stopping what was a horrific ordeal for the thirty or so donkeys involved in this festival, and that it was made possible by a united collaboration with other animal welfare associations. Now we can try and stop similar cases in Spain, helping to protect many more donkeys in the future.'

A happy ending

On 24th March 2010 El Refugio del Burrito took part in one of its biggest rescues to date – nearly thirty equines from Alora Malaga. Five of the animals were donkeys – three young males, all about twelve months old, and a mare with her six-month-old foal.

The donkeys, horses and ponies had been reported to the Agricultural Office of Alora Malaga by SEPRONA (the Spanish equivalent of the RSPCA) as they were living without proper fencing very close to a working railway track, which posed a real danger, both to the animals and, of course, the general public.

When the Agricultural Office investigated they also found that the animals' documentation was not up to date. Due to financial difficulties, the owner was unable to pay the fines imposed for this, and was unable to build proper stables and fencing. As a consequence, Alora's Agricultural Office took the animals; the donkeys were relinquished to El Refugio and the horses and ponies were taken to CYD Santa Maria, a refuge in Alhaurin el Grande.

It was an emotional day, especially for the owner. Although he didn't have the proper stabling and fencing he loved his animals very much, but he was happy that his donkeys were going to live at El Refugio, as it is near enough for him to visit as often as he likes.

Donkeys living happily at El Refugio's main farm in Fuente de Piedre

T

DONKEYS

Tacita

Our overseas staff see many sad cases, but we were particularly touched by the efforts of our whole team in Mexico to save the life of one little donkey called Tacita.

The Donkey Sanctuary's vet, Omar Prado Ortiz, who works in Mexico City, told us that a gentleman donkey owner, who was completely blind, called the clinic in desperation. His donkey had been killed by a wild dog, and her young foal, Tacita, was also savagely attacked but had survived. Tacita was in a terrible condition, with a very large wound on her head. Her owner travelled for twelve hours to get to the clinic, arriving at midnight. Omar and Horacio (Mexican Project Leader) were astonished that she was still alive. She was in a bad way and her left ear had to be removed completely. In a terrible state of shock Tacita soon lost all her hair, yet she continued to eat and remained determined to survive. Omar visited her every day to clean her wounds and it took almost two months for her to recover fully.

Tacita is now a beautiful donkey and has been re-homed at a horse ranch where the owners have a good reputation for looking after their animals. Here she is cared for like a pet and kept away from dogs. Omar commented, 'Tacita is a very strong little donkey and we are so glad we were able to help her – it makes our jobs so worthwhile.'

Tacita on arrival

Tacita has recovered well. Pictured here with our Public Relations Officer, Amanda Gordon

Teddy

Teddy is a dear little brown gelding who came into our care in 1993 when he was thirteen years old. Unfortunately he was born blind and his owner, after caring for him since he was six months old, decided that he would benefit from being with other donkeys with a similar disability. Our blind and partially-sighted donkeys live in a specially adapted barn at The Donkey Sanctuary, which has padding around the sides to prevent injuries if they bump into them.

Some of the visually impaired donkeys have companions who are fully sighted and, of course, we never separate them. Fortunately for Teddy he has a good friend named Lucky, a sighted donkey, who leads him around. Despite his disability Teddy is an amazing – and often quite naughty – donkey. He can open gates and doors when he thinks there's no-one around! The staff absolutely adore him, as he is so kind and gentle, and is extremely cute, although woe betide any donkey who tries to steal his food! Anyone watching him probably wouldn't realise he was blind, and it's very encouraging to see how much Teddy enjoys life.

Teddy

Theodore

Theodore

Many people love coming to see our Poitou donkeys, as they are so different to other donkeys. I look on them as the 'Shire horses' of the donkey species. Poitous are a breed of donkey that originated from the Poitou region of France, about three hundred miles south-west of Paris. They have long, thick coats, which become easily matted and need grooming regularly. They are much bigger than traditional donkeys.

A great favourite here is our gentle giant, Theodore. He came into our care in 2003 and is now living with our Poitou group. He loves being stroked and cuddled, and he would be very happy if he could be groomed every minute of every day! Theodore has a fantastic nature and has so much love to give.

Tierra

Tierra is an Andalucian donkey, who came into our care in 2003. At around 14hh she is a very large donkey – so much so that the staff have nicknamed her 'big bird' (from the children's television series)!

Her owner bought her as a foal when he was living in Spain and brought her back to England when he returned. Having been trained and broken to harness Tierra worked on her owner's farm in Gloucestershire, plough-ing, moving timber and performing other farm tasks. Teenagers with special

Tierra

needs worked at the farm and they worked with Tierra under her owner's supervision.

As a member of the Education and Activities Unit, Tierra is taken to shows as well as being part of E and A's experience days, particularly when older children are taking part. She's very friendly and inquisitive, but can be a bit of a baby if she hurts herself, shying away from the vets or vet nurses when they go to see her.

Timothy (1)

Timothy was apparently given as a present to a young village boy as a reward for passing his eleven-plus exam. The boy had always wanted a donkey and his father already had a small well-fenced paddock near a main road.

When Timothy arrived there was great delight amongst the family; the boy visited him every possible moment and they both got on really well. Then one evening the indescribable happened. A group of boys from the local school who had failed their exam, had become very jealous. As the boy was so attached to Timothy, they decided to attack him, and five of the boys, one armed with a carving knife, crept up to his field one evening. Timothy had no reason to be afraid of the boys and had no sense of danger. With four of the boys holding him down, the other one sliced savagely through one ear and then the other. In agonised terror Timothy flung them off and was still blundering around the field, with blood pouring from his wounds, when the unsuspecting owner arrived with his evening carrot. A vet was called, who managed to deaden the pain. Then came the police but, because the boys were so young a prosecution was not possible. The boy was heartbroken, as Timothy wouldn't let him – or anyone else – near.

His father was desperate and rang The Horse and Pony Protection Trust, who took Timothy away from the scene of his terror. His wounds were tended and, after a difficult period of time, the Trust persuaded a local farmer to put him in his field with some horses. Timothy, however, was no longer capable of being sociable with either people or animals and after a while the farmer had to advise the Trust that it was impossible for anyone to keep him. They realised they had a major temperament problem on their hands and rang us to see if we would take him, as we had so much experience with donkeys.

When Timothy arrived at the Sanctuary everyone was horrified at the sight of his poor damaged ears and, with his lips drawn back and his eyes red and angry, he was obviously emotionally disturbed. He was put into a loosebox and given some hay and a bran mash. Collecting the mash bucket half an hour later proved difficult; he reared up, with eyes blazing and teeth bared. After that no one was allowed to go into his stable alone.

Every trick was tried to gain his confidence, including introducing him to other geldings, but Timothy cared for them no more than people and often the prospective companion had to be rescued from the loosebox! It seemed the only answer was to put him to sleep, to erase the terrible memories forever.

Then a miracle happened! Two very fat chocolate-coloured donkeys called Henry and Henrietta came in and they were put in the stable next to Timothy. One night on my evening rounds I found Henry lying down, barely breath-

ing, having suffered a massive heart attack. I phoned for the vet, then I ran back to the stable with rugs to try and keep him warm. As I knelt beside him, massaging his heart to try to encourage the very weak beat, Henrietta became a real nuisance, even standing on Henry's inert form in an endeav-our to share what she thought was a pleasant stroking. I had no choice but to push her, protesting, into the corridor join-ing the stables together and she promptly vanished from view. By the time the vet arrived Henry was unconscious and, despite desperate attempts to save him, he died. I was so upset as I stumbled out into the corridor with tears in my eyes – but then I stopped in amazement. Timothy's head was extended over the door of the stable next door, and gently nuzzling him was Henrietta! I could not believe it! I gently opened Timothy's door and Henrietta walked into his stable calmly and continued the nuzzling.

After they had spent a few days together Timothy and Henrietta were let out into the yard. Henrietta led the way with Timothy quietly following her. This was a daily occur-rence until they were moved to a paddock of their own, although they were able to talk to the donkeys over the fence in the next field. Henrietta was very firm with Timothy; at the first sign of bared teeth she would push him away from the donkey he was talking to!

Timothy became great friends with Herb Fry, one of my first employees

The two friends lived happily together for many years before Henrietta died in 1990. Having calmed down and forgotten the horrors of his past, Timothy spent the next four years in Main Yard, being cuddled and cosseted by the Sanctuary's many visitors before his death at the grand old age of forty-three years.

Timothy (2)

Timothy was born in August 1999 and is a very handsome grey gelding. Along with a group of nine donkey friends he came into the care of The Donkey Sanctuary in 2004 when their loving and caring owners felt that, for personal reasons, they could no longer care for them. Timothy was the 9,034th admis-sion. He is very lively and is interested in everything and everybody! With his friendly nature and love of learning new things he was an ideal donkey to work with the children at the EST Sidmouth Centre. His love of human company is the main reason why he was chosen for the Adoption Scheme. His best friend is Walter.

Timothy is a clever donkey who always finds a way to get what he wants. He loves being groomed and never wants the groom to stop. As soon as she turns away he rushes into the arena and rolls on the floor, getting into an awful mess. Then he trots back to the groom asking to be brushed again! He often gets up to mischief, too. One bitterly cold winter's morning Hayley, one of the grooms, went into the shed to prepare the donkeys' feed. A strong gust of wind blew the door shut and when she went to open the door again she found that Timothy had pulled the bolt across with his teeth. She was locked in, and was there for at least twenty minutes before Claudia, who was passing by on her way to the office, heard her cries for help. The poor girl was frozen with cold and, through chattering teeth she told Claudia that this wasn't the first time Timothy had shut her in!

Timothy is a very handsome donkey!

Tiny Titch and So Shy

While I was at a meeting of The Donkey Breed Society in 1973 the name of Violet Philpin came up (see her story under 'P'). She was the subject of a fair amount of concern amongst council members, as she was very elderly and was looking after more than two hundred donkeys which she had bought in from dealers all over the country. Niels and I decided to visit her. A more dedicated and devoted person we could never meet; she loved every one of her charges. But what of their fate if anything happened to her? She must have been eighty-one on our first visit and she was in deep financial difficulties. She had trouble with the dealers from whom she bought her donkeys and we promised to help in any way we could.

Only an hour after we arrived home she phoned to ask if we could take six 'very bad' donkeys that had just been delivered from Reading market. She felt she just couldn't cope because they were in such a state, and she would send the lorry straight on to us, plus fifty pounds to help cover our costs. By 3 am the lorry arrived. On board were the donkeys we named Biddy, Black Beauty, Bill and Ben, So Shy and Tiny Titch. Their condition was indescribable – Niels and my eldest children, Lise and Paul, helped them into the biggest stable which I had emptied in readiness and we all stood quietly in the early morning light in shocked silence. None of the donkeys could move alone and their spirits seemed completely broken.

The lorry driver was sitting where we left him in the kitchen with a cup of coffee. I said, 'Poor little donkeys – they're in an awful condition.' 'Naw,' he replied. 'Reading market isn't as bad as Southall – you should see 'em there! They'll be all right in a week or so – you'll see'. 'You should be ashamed to even transport them,' I replied. He stood up in a menacing fashion. 'Hey, I'm just the driver and they're just bloody donkeys. Get off my back', and he left the kitchen without drinking his coffee.

Niels and the children were still talking quietly to the donkeys, feeding each a little bran mash. We only dared let them have a morsel as too much can cause severe colic and in any event it was all they could manage. The slight interest shown on being given a warm meal was enough reward for all of us for the night so we turned out the light and a very subdued and sad family got to sleep around 4 am.

There was the usual early morning dash to get breakfast and get the children off to school and it was eight o'clock before I was ready to go out to see the donkeys again. Herb Fry, my helper, was waiting for me at the back door, his kindly face wrinkled up with concern. From being a young boy he had always worked on farms and been with animals. To him farm animals had a simple purpose in life. They were bred carefully, reared properly and when their time came they were culled for human consumption. This was the way of the farmer, and Herb fully approved.

In the morning light we stood looking at the donkeys. 'Tisn't right,' he said. 'Look at that poor little beggar's back.' The smallest donkey was shivering in the corner – his back was bent from cowering at the frequent beatings that had been his lot and the hair looked solid and peculiar. The solid lumps on Tiny Titch were pieces of sacking embedded in his back, with small broken pieces of spine showing through. He was only about eight months old. I cried and so did

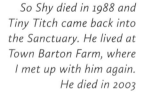

So Shy died in 1988 and Tiny Titch came back into the Sanctuary. He lived at Town Barton Farm, where I met up with him again. He died in 2003

Herb. Could Tiny Titch stand the anaesthetic the vet would need to give him to remove the sacking and could we mend his splintered spine? We decided to let him recover a little first, and put him in one of the smallest stables with a poor little thin terrified mare, So Shy.

With the vet and Herb's help I was able to touch So Shy gently and look at her teeth to estimate her age. *All* her front teeth were broken, congested blood still on the gums. She had been beaten as badly as Tiny Titch. The vet gave her an anaesthetic straight away, as she could not possibly eat with her mouth in that condition. We removed five chipped and broken teeth and sewed up her lacerated gums. The only good thing was that they were her milk teeth and, with luck, new ones would replace them. We covered her with a rug and stroked her gently until she came round from the anaesthetic.

Luckily the other donkeys in the group were not in such a bad condition and they made a slow but sure recovery.

There was a happy ending to this story – So Shy and Tiny Titch recovered fully with us – and fell quietly in love! When they were better I found them a wonderful home in Devon and arranged with the new owners that Tiny Titch be gelded when he was ready, and the Sanctuary would pay. They did this when he was two, but just a little too late! So Shy produced a foal, Rosy, one year later!

Toby

Toby is a pale grey gelding with a dark cross on his back. He was born in 1997 and had lived on a farm within Alton Towers. When the farm closed in 2002 he and another donkey named Tufty came to live at The Donkey Sanctuary.

Toby was used to lots of visitors at the farm and he really enjoyed all the love and attention he received from them. His excellent temperament made him ideal to work with children with special needs and disabilities, so both donkeys were transferred to the EST Manchester Centre. Children and staff alike both adore them and Toby was chosen as one of the donkeys available for EST's Adoption Scheme.

A clever donkey like Toby will always find a way to get what he wants – especially if it is edible. He proved this one day when, standing in his pen waiting for his turn in the arena, he spotted a sweet on the floor outside. He could not reach it by leaning over the barrier, so he got down on his knees, put his head through the gate and, with a flick of his tongue, got his prize. Delicious! See photo overleaf.

Toto

Toto was rescued and taken to one of our holding bases in France, before being re-homed at El Refugio del Burrito in 2003, when he was one year old. Toto is a very smart and lively donkey with huge ears. He is a member of El Refugio's

Toby

ABOVE RIGHT *Toto's large ears are impressive!*

donkey assisted riding therapy group for children with special needs and became the newest donkey in the Adoption Scheme in 2010.

Twink and Ami

Ami is an Andalucian donkey, who came into The Donkey Sanctuary's care with her young son, Oaty, as their owner could no longer afford to keep them.

Andalucian donkeys were bred to meet the requirements of the Andalucian farmers in Spain who needed a steady, willing, patient and well-developed animal that could also be used to produce mules, which were in much demand. They worked in the cork forests and olive and citrus groves. Unfortunately, mechanisation has resulted in the breed dramatically diminishing in numbers to the point where it is now considered to be an endangered species.

Twink is a very shy, small donkey. She was sent in with three other donkeys quite a while ago by an animal welfare group that could no longer afford to keep them. By chance all these donkeys ended up in the same group at Woods Farm, and Twink and Ami immediately fell in love with each other, despite their difference in size!

Twink and Ami; good friends despite their difference in size!

DONKEY FACTS, PEOPLE AND PLACES

Tanzania

Donkeys are the most important animals for transport and farming in Tanzania but, as a result of severe rural poverty, they suffer from undernourishment, lack of appropriate or affordable harness, poor carts (designed for oxen), poor knowledge of welfare and negative cultural beliefs. Beating and overloading are common.

In the last few years we have provided funding to some local animal welfare groups which are helping them.

We support the Tanzania Animal Protection Organisation (TAPO), which carried out a three-month welfare education programme in 2010 in the Kahama district of the Shinyanga region. Around seven hundred donkey owners and handlers were given training in basic donkey care including feeding, shelter and hoof care. There were also field demonstrations on good harnessing practice.

We also help fund the Tanzania Animal Welfare Society (TAWESO), which is running a Donkey Welfare Education Project in the Mpwapwa district of central Tanzania, and the Arusha Society for the Protection of Animals (ASPA), which is running an education programme for school children and communities.

A typical scene on a market day in Tanzania

In addition, we funded a training programme for donkey owners run by the Sokoine University of Agriculture – this was so successful that the donkey owners went on to form their own group.

Turks and Caicos

In 1991 the government and local people in the Turks and Caicos Islands asked me for assistance with a problem they had with regard to the feral donkeys and horses on the island of Grand Turk. In the past donkeys were used to carry salt from the lakes on the island, but they were abandoned when the commercial viability of the industry failed. Over the years the donkeys had become feral and increased enormously in number.

The problem was that, when the dry season came many donkeys died as the waterholes dried up, and others wandered into the town looking for water and food. Of course the clever donkeys soon worked out a few things, which made government action imperative. Each house by law had to collect any rainfall during the year, and they have plastic drainpipes from their roofs leading into water storage tanks. The donkeys worked out that if they kicked hard enough at the drainpipe they could get plenty of water. They became so clever at it that the islanders became desperate and the government decided to ship the donkeys to Haiti for meat. The islanders weren't happy about this and The Donkey Sanctuary's assistance was sought.

I was met by a minister responsible for the donkey project and taken to meet the governor of the island and a small committee which had been set up to deal with the problem. It was agreed that, with the assistance of funding from The Donkey Sanctuary, a large area of land would be fenced, and shelter and water provided. All the donkeys would be rounded up and brought into the compound.

Apparently children were asked to do the job of rounding the donkeys up and putting them in the compound, and for this they were paid one pound per donkey. However, I was amused to hear reports that, once there became a shortage of donkeys living in the wild, the children began sneaking donkeys back out of the compound and bringing them back in again to claim another payment!

The Donkey Sanctuary arranged for fifty of the donkeys to be flown to Jamaica to work with local horticultural farmers carrying their crops to roads accessible for trucks. These donkeys are regularly monitored today. The Sanctuary also agreed to send a team of vets to Grand Turk to castrate as many stallions as possible to prevent further breeding.

In 2008 we learned that feral donkeys on Salt Cay (another of the Turks and Caicos Islands) were causing difficulties. Proposed development of the island, including the building of hotels and golf courses, meant that plans were allegedly being made, once again, to round the donkeys up and ship them to Haiti for meat, and there was huge concern for their welfare during shipment. So, as I write this, we are again helping the government of the islands to find a better way.

Donkeys in Turks and Caicos

U

DONKEYS

Ug

Ug came into our care with his friend, Jenny, in November 1995. Their previous owner's circumstances had changed, including a house move, and he decided to send the donkeys to The Donkey Sanctuary.

At forty-four years old Ug is the oldest donkey at East Axnoller Farm. He's a typical old gentleman and very stuck in his ways! He likes a choice of breakfast, frequently changing his mind as to what he fancies on any particular day. He doesn't like taking his medication, and the staff have to be very inventive to find ways to hide it in his food!

Ug – we don't know why he was given such a strange name!

Uncle Moses

Uncle Moses came in with pony friend Sooty in 2004 due to a change in their owner's circumstances, and they live at East Axnoller Farm.

As you will see from the photograph, Uncle Moses is a very hairy grey donkey! At thirty-one years old he's determined that at his time of life he should get most of the staff's attention, especially at grooming time. He has a unique-sounding bray, which he uses to his advantage – in fact his voice is so loud they've decided it's better to groom him first, rather than suffer his excited noise!

Uncle Moses

Uncle Sam

On 4th July 1973 Uncle Sam was born as a first foal to Dusty and her male companion Parsley. He was followed three years later by his sister, Dixie. They all lived on a farm in West Wales and were much-loved by their owner, Mrs Barnard. However, due to a house move, she couldn't keep them any longer and they came into our care in 1999.

As a youngster Uncle Sam could be difficult, but was very clever. He learned how to undo the kitchen door, untie knots, and let himself and his family in and out of places they shouldn't be! According to Mrs Barnard the local community used to rally round and help retrieve the wanderers whenever they escaped.

Uncle Sam

Since relinquishing her donkeys, Mrs Barnard visits Town Barton Farm once a year for a whole week. She told the staff that when the donkeys were living on her farm she used to whistle to them in the evenings to get them in from the field. She proved it by standing outside Town Barton's Oldies Barn and whistling. True enough, they came running across the barn with Uncle Sam in the lead! They'd remembered – and it was a very emotional moment for everyone.

DONKEY FACTS, PEOPLE AND PLACES

USA

The donkey is the symbol of the Democratic Party of the United States of America. This originated in a cartoon by Thomas Nast, a nineteenth century political cartoonist who worked for *Harper's Weekly*. Nast also depicted the elephant as the symbol of the Republican Party.

A brooch I purchased in the USA

DONKEYS

Val

An arrival at The Irish Sanctuary in 1990 was Val. She had the worst feet we'd ever seen at the time, with the hoofs completely twisted round. The neglect of donkeys' feet causes more actual suffering to the animal than any other single item. When the hooves are allowed to grow without attention they change the whole stance of the animal, stretching tendons past their maximum and often causing permanent lameness even after treatment.

After a period of careful farriery treatment Val's hoofs were returned to normal, although it took her a long time to learn to walk again without pain.

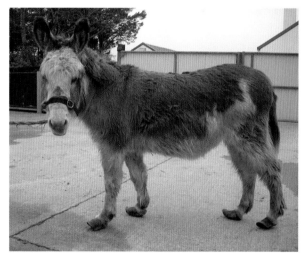

Walking was very painful for Val

Venere and Holly

Venere was rescued by Il Rifugio Degli Asinelli from a donkey breeding centre in southern Italy. She was in a terrible condition and needed the Sanctuary's expert care.

Donkey breeding centres are commonly found in Italy where there is a great demand for their meat. Venere was used solely to produce foals and it is not known how many years she was 'worked'. A local animal welfare charity, Nata Libera, became aware that the centre, in Teramo, was experiencing financial difficulties. The owners agreed to release Venere to Il Rifugio and the charity asked that other donkeys in a very bad condition should be taken too. Holly

Venere (left) *and Holly* (right) *at Il Rifugio with their carers, Denise and Marianna*

was one of them. She had a bite wound on her nose which was severely infected and later needed plastic surgery to correct its form and function.

Barbara Massa, who manages Il Rifugio, recalls the story when Venere was found. 'This poor little donkey was quite elderly and, as her feet were so overgrown, she couldn't walk down the hill to get to drinking water at the river.'

Venere took some time to settle in to her new surroundings, and had great difficulty in standing properly. She was also nearly blind. Barbara explained that Venere was understandably difficult to handle when she first arrived. She would kick anyone who came anywhere near her and she hated having her hooves cleaned. After a while she calmed down and eventually would lift her foot in response to a touch on her leg!

Unfortunately, after only a few years of peace and contentment at Il Rifugio it was apparent that her health and her quality of life were deteriorating and, in July 2010, a decision was made to put her to sleep.

Holly has now made a full recovery; she is six years old and enjoying the company of Ombra, her best friend.

DONKEY FACTS, PEOPLE AND PLACES

Top veterinary award for donkey hospital

The Donkey Sanctuary has an excellent veterinary hospital designed specifically for treating donkeys and I was delighted when our Veterinary Department was awarded Tier 2 Hospital Status in October 2009. Facilities include an operating theatre with closed circuit anaesthesia and diagnostic equipment including endoscopy, X-ray and ultrasound.

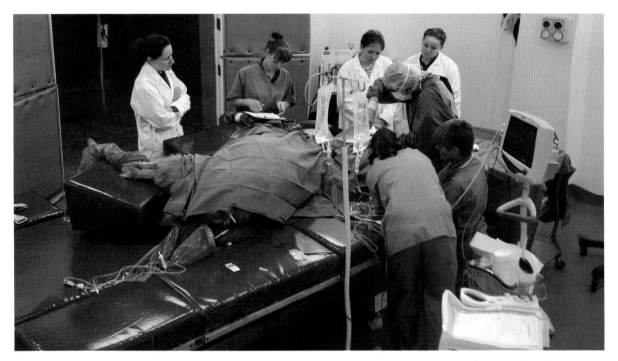

The operating theatre at the hospital

The Royal College of Veterinary Surgeons Practice Standards Scheme was launched in January 2005. It is a voluntary scheme which aims to promote and maintain high standards of veterinary care. Some of the areas which undergo rigorous inspection are patient care, equipment, facilities, staff and safety procedures. Our Director of Veterinary Services, Andrew Trawford, says, 'The Veterinary Department was given a good report. Acquiring Tier 2 status is a major achievement for the department and represents significant hard work by everyone.'

The donkey vicar

Contributed by the Reverend Peter Leverton

It was in September 1994 and I had been officially retired for nearly three years. I was sitting in my study trying to sort out what my computer was up to, when I received a telephone call from a lady who asked if I would be willing to take a Memorial Service at The Donkey Sanctuary. She said my name had been given to her by Reverend David Robottom, the vicar of Salcombe Regis who had conducted the first Memorial Service, but who had now moved to a new parish. I said yes, I would be only too pleased. The lady was Dr Elisabeth Svendsen, and that phone call added a very interesting dimension to my ministry as a priest.

I met Dr Svendsen, and we discussed the service, which was the second of what would turn out to be an annual event to be held on 4 October, the Feast

Rev Lev with one of the Sanctuary's donkeys

Day of St Francis of Assisi, the patron saint of animals. It turned out to be a very moving day. The service took place in a large marquee, and during the singing of the hymns donkeys were walked around the congregation, to the great enjoyment of all present. After the service Dr Svendsen and I climbed into what she called the 'vicarmobile', a vehicle with an open back, where we stood as we travelled around the Sanctuary. I had prayers with the people who were waiting for us at their particular memorials, which I blessed; these can be trees or benches along the Sanctuary walks, or a plaque on the wall in memory of a loved one, or a precious pet.

After the service someone came up to me and said, 'That was a very nice service but you didn't mention the donkeys!' I knew a little about donkeys as my eldest daughter owned one with a pony and my other children loved animals, but I decided to learn more about the work of The Donkey Sanctuary! The following year I was able to include its work in my address and prayers.

I won't go on about the following years except to say that the date was changed to the Saturday nearest St Francis' Day because so many people who wished to attend were unable to come on a week-day. Then in October 2000 I had to conduct the service sitting down as I was recovering from two serious operations and the people came to me instead of us going to them. Once, while on my usual round of visiting the office staff, as I approached I heard a voice I knew quite well say, 'Watch out – here comes Rev Lev' and we all had a good laugh. The name caught on I'm now known to everyone at the Sanctuary as 'Rev Lev'!

Donkey Week is another annual event at the Sanctuary. I've met hundreds of 'Donkey Weekers' over the year, and in 2000 Dr Svendsen and I decided to hold a special service on the Sunday. This was first held at Sidmouth Parish Church and later at the beautiful country church at Tedburn St Mary, right next to the Sanctuary's farm, Town Barton.

In December 2001 The Donkey Sanctuary held its very first 'Candlelight Evening'. This was a magical evening, with over twelve thousand candles flickering around the Sanctuary, lit in memory of supporters' loved ones. What a lovely sight! The service was held in the open area of the yard. It was freezing cold, but we loved hearing the donkeys joining in the hymns. The next year the service was held in New Barn, which was much warmer and the numbers of people attending had trebled. In 2009 it was reported that two thousand people attended the service. The Ross-on-Wye Town Band played for us, there was a Santa's Grotto, and mince pies and mulled wine were available. Fifteen thousand candles decorated the Sanctuary's grounds – it was a really wonderful occasion with everyone going home laughing and singing.

Visitors

As The Donkey Sanctuary has grown in size so has the number of visitors. Many millions of people have come to see the donkeys over the years. It really is a lovely place to visit – donkeys quietly grazing against a backdrop of rolling fields and the sea.

I've met so many nice people during my forty years with the donkeys. The first television interview nearly ended in disaster, with Bob Forbes of BBC Radio Devon (see story of Angelina under 'A'). Then Angela Rippon came along and did a wonderful half hour programme for the BBC which really put the Sanctuary on the map!

Over the years we've had many special visitors, including two Royal visits. Princess Anne (the Princess Royal) came to see The Slade Centre and its work in 1985 and, more recently, the Earl and Countess of Wessex shared their time between the Sanctuary and the Centre (by then known as the EST Sidmouth Centre).

Film and television stars who have come to see us over the years include Virginia McKenna, Arthur Negus, Ant and Dec and Dame Thora Hird (a very special lady who did us the honour of opening our Leeds EST Centre in 1998).

Dame Thora Hird enjoyed coming to see the donkeys and was a great supporter of our work

On the other hand, I remember one occasion when our Visitors' Centre received a call from the police who had been warned by a coach driver that he was bringing three 'families from hell' to the Sanctuary. The families had apparently already caused havoc in Sidmouth! Members of staff prepared themselves for the onslaught. The main concerns were protection of the donkeys and possible shoplifting. However, they were surrounded by so many watchful staff when they arrived that it was impossible for them to get up to too much mischief. Everyone breathed a sigh of relief when they left. Luckily this is a very rare occurrence!

Visitors are not charged admission or car parking fees. I've always felt that those people who donate towards the care of the donkeys should be allowed to see how their money is being spent without having to pay for the privilege! I think many people come along expecting to see a dotty little old lady with lots of dirty sheds and old, scraggy tired-looking donkeys! They get quite a surprise to find a beautiful, peaceful and pristine-clean Sanctuary with excellent, friendly staff and delightful well cared-for donkeys.

Little Pippa enjoyed meeting Connie when she visited the Sanctuary

DONKEYS

Wayne

Wayne is a skewbald gelding, who was born in 1996. He was taken into The Donkey Sanctuary's care in 2004 with his donkey companion, Garth. Both donkeys had previously been bought by a very kind couple who had been concerned for their welfare.

Wayne was the 8,992nd entry and, although at first he and Garth were a little nervous, they soon settled down. The staff who looked after them soon realised that, with Wayne's love of people and his gentle, friendly nature, he would be ideal to work with children. He's a very happy donkey who enjoys both working and playing, and for this reason he was chosen to join the EST Ivybridge's Outreach programme and as a member of the Adoption Scheme.

The staff firmly believe that Wayne would like to live by the sea! With some time to fill between visits to residential homes in Cornwall, he was taken to Portreath beach for a paddle. Needless to say he loved it, kicking about in the sand and playing with the seaweed – then standing looking out to sea, almost mesmerised by the waves and enjoying the sea air.

Wayne is available to adopt from EST Ivybridge

William

William is a tri-colour gelding, born in 1993, who was taken into The Donkey Sanctuary's care in 1996. He and another donkey, Teddy, were rescued by a kind lady, who realised that their previous owner was neglecting them.

Although she wanted to keep them herself she realised this would not be possible, as she had many other animals to care for and had insufficient land. Teddy, who was a lot older than William, passed away in 2003.

William soon settled on one of our outlying farms and quickly regained both his health and a very cheeky personality! He is lively, interested in everything and everybody and it was obvious that he would benefit from working with disadvantaged children. He is very popular with children and staff alike at the EST Leeds Centre; he's a real 'home-lover, as he doesn't enjoy travelling very much, so he's always seen at the Centre ready to take the children for a ride or greet visitors, particularly those who have 'adopted' him. His greatest pleasures are having his ears scratched and having an afternoon siesta!

William is a great favourite at EST Leeds

DONKEY FACTS, PEOPLE AND PLACES

War

Donkeys have been used throughout history during wartime for transportation of supplies and pulling equipment, as well as carrying people.

A famous example of how useful a donkey could be is the story of John Simpson Kirkpatrick. During the First World War Private Kirkpatrick had served with the 3rd Field Ambulance Australian Army Medical Corps in Gallipoli. He was known as the 'Man with the Donkey' because of his rescue missions, leading a donkey carrying wounded soldiers from the front line. He became a familiar sight on the battlefield, but sadly his heroism was short-lived when he was killed by machine-gun fire in May 1915. He was mentioned in dispatches for gallant and distinguished service in the field and was posthumously awarded the first Anzac Commemorative Medallion.

Reports of appalling cruelty to donkeys and mules in war zones have shocked people for many years. It could be reasoned that, when hearing of the numerous suicide bombers who cause death and destruction in today's uncertain times, it is the person's choice to take his or her life as well as that of others. However, several reports in the media have suggested that 'donkey suicide bombing' has been taking place. Donkeys have been loaded with explosives and placed in positions to cause the most harm and, once in place, the explosives have been detonated. This has happened in several war zones, including Afghanistan and Iraq.

To remember the many animals killed in wars a memorial has been erected in Park Lane in London. The main dedication reads:

This monument is dedicated to all the animals that served and died along-side British and allied forces in wars and campaigns throughout time.

A smaller inscription reads:

They had no choice.

Along with other animal lovers, my name is inscribed on the back of the monument

Worry

It's cold and dark, and I'm standing alone
On a wet, boggy pasture I have to call home
If I try to lie down my coat gets all wet
And although I am freezing, I'm covered in sweat.

I'm worried

I'm not sure why, but I've pain in my feet
I've turned right around so my back's to the sleet
But my legs are all shaky and I just cannot stand
And sink to the ground to lie on the land.

I'm frightened

I'm scared that I won't be alive for the dawn
I'm starving, with no chance to eat till the morn
And sleep seems impossible, I'm so very cold
I'm not very big, and I don't think I am old.

I'm shivering

I think I am dreaming – I see a bright light
And I hear people's voices, coming near in the night
'He must be near here – it's where he was seen'
And the footsteps come nearer – I'm lit up in a beam.

I'm startled

'Oh my God, here he is, in a terrible state
I just hope we've found him before it's too late'.
And gentle hands lift me, I just cannot stand
And they carry me off over wet, boggy land.

And I'm worried again

I cannot remember the rest of the night
I rested on straw as we drove until light
Then tender hands lifted me out of the van
And a kind voice said 'try to stand if you can'.

And I tried

I was helped to a stable, so warm and so clean
Given hay and water – the best meal I've seen
And they bathed my feet and I felt this was heaven
For God had found me sanctuary in Devon.

And I never had to worry again!

Taken from Not Just Donkeys
by Dr Elisabeth D Svendsen and reproduced by
kind permission of Whittet Books Ltd

DONKEYS

Xanthoulla

On 10th September 2008 The Cyprus Donkey Sanctuary received a call from a government veterinary inspector about a donkey that was found wandering in Armenochori village in the Limassol District. We asked her to report it to the local Muchtar (Mayor) of the village and to the police so that they could try to find the owner.

Despite their best efforts, the owner could not be found so the inspector asked if we could collect the donkey, as she had obviously been abandoned. She was brought to the Sanctuary on 17th September and named 'Xanthoulla' after the inspector who helped rescue her.

Xanthoulla is around twenty-two years old and was probably a working donkey. She had some sore areas below her eyes which were probably caused

Xanthoulla

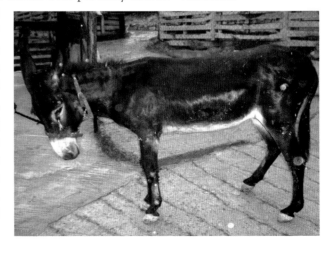

by flies. These were treated and soon looked much better. She was transferred to one of our holding bases at Sterako in May 2009, where she lives in peace and contentment with fifteen other donkeys. She has lots of space to run and roll in the dirt. The staff were concerned when, towards the end of 2009, she started losing weight but a full veterinary examination and a dental check revealed no reason for this. She was given extra feed to bring her weight up and ensure she was the correct condition score. She has progressed nicely and is now an ideal condition score 3.

Xavier, Mudge, Osborn and McCloud

A farmer in Northern Ireland decided he didn't want six of his colt foals and they were taken into our holding base in Strabane, County Tyrone, run by one of our Welfare Officers, Marie McCormack. Since they arrived in 2009 the six donkeys remained at the holding base, but in August 2010 four were brought over to the UK. Two remain in Northern Ireland.

Xavier with his friends

Xenophon

Xenophon was a working donkey in a village near Agros, in the Limassol district. Born around 1992, he was used for working in the fields, carrying panniers of grapes and olives for his owner. Unfortunately his owner fell and broke her leg very badly, ending up in hospital. As is often the case nowadays, the lady's family didn't live close by and were unable to look after her donkey. She was also finding it very difficult to get a farrier to trim his hooves, which had now become rather long, and so she asked The Donkey Sanctuary (Cyprus) if we would take him into care.

Xenophon

There was an additional request – his owner also looked after and worked another donkey belonging to a friend of hers. Both of them were very good friends and had formed a strong bond. As she couldn't look after either of the donkeys, both owners sensibly asked if we could take the two of them, so that they wouldn't be separated. Some bonded donkeys can get very stressed if taken away from each other and this stress can cause health problems.

So on 14th October 2010 off we went to collect both of them. A family member met us to sign the paperwork and after a little reluctance, both donkeys went on the trailer to travel back to Vouni.

Not surprisingly, neither donkey had a name and so our Office Manager came up with Xenophon for one of them. Xenaphon was a Greek horseman who is often referred to as the forefather of modern classical riding. This then led to thinking about Alexander the Great and his horse, Bucephalus. Guess what we called our second donkey? A little too 'upmarket' for our two friends? We certainly don't think so!

DONKEY FACTS, PEOPLE AND PLACES

X-rays

June Evers is my greatest friend! We met on our first day at the Princess Mary High School in Halifax in 1935, both shivering with fright as we stood in front of the huge wooden school door. In those days parents didn't come in with you on the first day and, at five years old, it was a really terrifying ordeal.

Until we were nine years old we stayed together at the school, but when the war started I was moved to a school nearer home in Brighouse in Yorkshire. However, June and I remained close friends, meeting at weekends and staying at each other's homes.

While I went on to college to train as a teacher, June trained as a radiographer, but we always kept in touch and, after my husband left me in 1981, June came to live with me. By now she had progressed and was Superintendent of Radiography at Exeter's largest hospital, the Royal Devon and Exeter.

June stood her turn doing night duty and I decided to register as a volunteer to give her a hand. When I had finished my 'donkey work' I used to go to the hospital at about eight in the evening, often staying until four or five the following morning. Some nights were very quiet and I spent my time helping June by typing out the following day's appointments and finding the appropriate X-rays of the patients who would be attending. Other nights were extremely busy.

June and I have many memories of those days, some of which continue to be a great source of amusement even now. I remember wheeling a semiconscious woman along on a trolley when she suddenly grabbed my hand and asked, 'I'm dead, aren't I?' 'No,' I replied. 'You're in hospital and being taken for an X-ray.' 'I don't believe you,' she said. 'You're Mrs Svendsen and I always prayed that when I died I could come and live with you and the donkeys'!

On another busy Saturday night the porters brought in four men on trolleys. At the bottom end of each trolley was a policeman's helmet. The men had been injured in a brawl following a football match in Exeter. While I was registering them for X-rays I was pleased to see that the Chief Constable had come along to see how they were. It must have comforted them enormously.

I've left June's favourite story for her to tell you:

'During the years I was a radiographer Betty would sometimes come to give me a hand when I was on night duty. She would carry the cassettes, chat to the patients and so on. Then she graduated to driving the mobile X-ray machine when we had to go on the wards. She particularly enjoyed positioning the machine to drive through the middle of the special doors which would swing open under pressure and allow her to sail triumphantly into the ward.

One evening she set off with my colleague for the wards. They returned sometime later looking somewhat stunned. It seems that Betty had, as usual, confidently approached the ward doors and, with perhaps more pressure than normal had driven forward, only to discover that these doors were not of the swing variety. So it was to the sound of breaking glass and splintering wood that she surged into the room.

To everyone's amazement the patient in the bed opposite the doors, who until then had been in a comatose state, shot up in bed. He subsequently made a full recovery, which of course Betty and I put down to her spectacular entry into his room. We were, however, surprised that no-one ever complained about the damage caused!'

June and I have been friends for many years!

DONKEYS

Yetty

Yetty was relinquished to our Irish Sanctuary in March 2000 and, due to lack of space, was brought over to Devon in September 2007. He joined another donkey, Benjamin, in a foster home the following year. Unfortunately they had to be returned to the Sanctuary in July 2008, and Benjamin subsequently passed away.

In April 2010 Yetty was fostered out to a new home to be a companion to one of our foster donkeys named Thistle, whose previous companion, Chloe, had recently died. Yetty settled in extremely well and became very close to Thistle. His new foster owner, Mrs Childs, told us, 'Thistle was always a bit of a bully to Chloe, but he has met his match with Yetty and there is no longer any need to separate them at feeding time. They go everywhere together and they tolerate the Jacob's sheep that live very close by. He is becoming tamer by the day and enjoys taking carrots and apples.'

Area Welfare Officer Penny Tobin, tells me that Yetty enjoys running around the paddock and not coming near when she visits! She says, 'He is a very strong character and has certainly settled in well with Thistle. Yetty likes to think he is the boss and in control of the other donkey and the people who care for him. He is *not* a pushover! He is food motivated and likes to keep everyone on their toes. He started his life with Mrs Childs with a roll in the mud and continues to enjoy making his coat muddy, dirty and wet – especially after a groom or a wash!

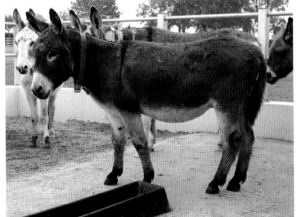

Yetty

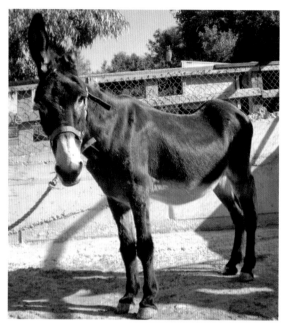

Yiannis doesn't seem to mind having only one ear!

Yiannis One Ear

Yiannis One Ear had been taken in by The Donkey Sanctuary (Cyprus)'s former owners, Patrick and Mary Skinner. He came into care as he was unwanted by his owner. As his name suggests, he only has one ear, the other having been sliced off in an act of revenge by a prospective purchaser because he had been outbid by someone else and he didn't want to pay a higher price. As a consequence the owner wasn't able to sell him for the price that had been offered by the other man. As a disfigured animal no one would want to buy him, so he was sent into the Sanctuary.

Yiannis is around twenty-six years old and comes over to the fence to see visitors despite the trauma caused by a human being in the past. Bless him, he is a bit of a strange shape in that he looks as though he was made of spare parts! It can be quite difficult to get a rug to fit him in the winter, which he needs as he seems to feel the cold. He also avoids going out in the rain as the water goes down the hole where his ear was, but he is quite happy to stay in the barn on rainy days. He also loves having his ear hole rubbed and it never ceases to amaze us that animals that have suffered severe trauma can be so forgiving and enjoy human company.

Yves, Wilfred and Moto

These three stallions were bred in Scotland by their previous owner but, as his property was being sold, it was necessary to find a new home for them all. In August 2010 they were taken to a holding base run by Jean Flint in Perthshire until such time as it is possible to bring them down to Devon.

All three donkeys are under four years old, and their future will be decided later. They could be suitable for fostering to a new home, or perhaps working in one of our EST Centres – or spending their lives living happily on one of the Sanctuary's farms.

Yves at Jean Flint's holding base

DONKEYS

Zebedee

Zebedee was relinquished to The Donkey Sanctuary in 2004. His owner had only had him for a year but she felt that, as he was so nervous, he would benefit from receiving training at The Donkey Sanctuary.

At first he lived at the Derbyshire Centre (formerly Newton Farm). He was indeed a very nervous donkey and he particularly disliked his ears being touched. Once he had settled in, though, he became more relaxed and confident, and the staff at the Centre thought he would be an ideal donkey for

Zebedee at EST Birmingham

working with children with special needs and disabilities at one of the EST Centres. He was moved to Birmingham EST in 2005.

Zebedee now enjoys working in the riding arena and loves most of all to trot during the rides, which always makes the children laugh.

Zebina and Tamarón

One of the 'in-foal' mares who came into our care in 2000 as a result of a joint RSPCA/Donkey Sanctuary rescue was Zebina. She was the last of the group left to foal and, as she grew fatter and fatter we spent many hours watching her in case there were problems. The vets were concerned, but we decided to wait and let nature take its course.

On the morning of 28th June, accompanied by my son, Paul, I was driving back from London having attended a reception at the Spanish Embassy the previous evening and, when we arrived at the Sanctuary, we drove up the track to Zebina's stable and field – and what a joyous sight greeted us! There she was, standing in the field cleaning her little jet black filly foal, who was literally only a few minutes old! We both nearly cried! There had been no problem with the birth; perhaps the extra time and care Zebina had received since coming into our care had enabled her to make up for her previous lack of nourishment.

Having been so kindly received by the Spanish Ambassador and his wife the previous evening (we discussed what could be done about the annual fiesta in Villanueva de la Vera), I decided to give the foal their family name, so Tamarón she became. Tamarón later made friends with Bandy, and the two donkeys joined a foster home in 2004.

Zebina with her foal, Tamarón

Zebina too was fostered to a new home with her friends Black Moll, Lady and Emma, but they came back to us in October 2006 as their foster carer had passed away unexpectedly. Another home has not yet been found for them, as it's difficult to find someone who is willing to take on a group of donkeys.

Zena

Zena was the last foal to be born to one of the pregnant mares who came from Scotland in 2009. Her mother, Flora, gave birth prematurely later the same year.

The staff found the foal curled up in the corner of the stable at 6.30 one morning. She was very quiet and obviously not well. We soon realised her back legs were not working properly and she could not stand up or walk. For the first week staff worked round the clock to help Zena stand up and reach her mother's udder for milk; it's very important that a foal receives its mother's milk within hours of its birth to ensure it receives the vital colostrum. Sometimes she wouldn't suckle so the staff combined bottle feeding with trying to encourage her to feed from her mother. Helping Zena to stand was a very good form of physiotherapy and this and the feeding regime was needed every two hours in the first weeks of her life.

Zena when first born

Happily, after two weeks Zena's legs became strong enough for her to walk and feed for herself and today she is a normal, happy little donkey! If it had not been for the intervention of our staff she would probably not be with us today.

Zena back to normal

DONKEY FACTS, PEOPLE AND PLACES

Zainab

Zainab is a little girl who was born with liver disease and at only twelve months old had to undergo a life-saving liver transplant operation. She was lucky enough to receive a liver from a young donor but disaster struck when it stopped working twelve hours after the procedure. Her mum, Aliya watched helplessly as doctors entered into a race against time to find another liver and her tiny daughter was put on life support and dialysis as her kidneys began to fail. At the last minute, a liver was found from an older donor. This was not an ideal match but with time running out, Zainab's doctors knew that any further delay would leave them unable to do the transplant.

Zainab thoroughly enjoys her contact with the donkeys

Aliya told us, 'If Zainab hadn't been given that second liver she probably wouldn't be here today. I am so grateful to the donor and would love more people to think about becoming organ donors.'

Zainab began the slow road to recovery at Birmingham Children's Hospital, starting with two weeks of procedures to close the incision which had been made right across her stomach, leaving her muscles very weak. While looking for ways to help her daughter's recovery, Aliya was told about the EST Manchester Centre, and Zainab has been attending weekly sessions for the last eighteen months. Riding the donkeys has led to significant strengthening in Zainab's stomach muscles, core stability and co-ordination.

The benefits of donkey riding therapy are not just physical. Zainab loves coming along to the Centre – it's the highlight of her week. Aliya says, 'Coming to EST has improved Zainab's confidence enormously. When she was very ill we weren't able to get out very often and she was very nervous about meeting people because of her hospital treatments. She was worried about what people were going to do to her, but everybody is very kind here and she is learning to trust new people.'

Aliya finds her visits to EST a welcome break from the worry of constant hospital visits. The staff are very understanding of her and Zainab's needs and she enjoys meeting other parents in a safe, friendly environment.

Zeedonks

Zeedonks are usually the offspring of a male zebra and a female donkey. They are also sometimes known as zonks or zonkeys. There are examples of these around the world today, although they are quite rare as, due to the differences in a donkey's chromosones (it has 62) and those of the zebra, which vary according to species, it is quite difficult to actually produce offspring.

A zeedonk (Photograph courtesy of Jennifer L. Schiff)

A final word

I really hope that you've enjoyed this book, with its many donkey stories and interesting anecdotes. With so many millions of donkeys in the world I'm sure I could add many more to my alphabetical list as our work continues – as it will for 'donkeys' years'!

INDEX

Page numbers in *italics* refer to illustrations